The Revd Dr Cally Hammond is t⸗ Caius College, Cambridge. She beg⸗ Classicist, first at Oxford and then ⸗ research on the Roman historians ⸗ought ⸗er the value of stories and narratives as a way of communicating truths and beliefs. This has stood her in good stead when thinking about the Gospels and the early Church. As well as working in academic life in Oxford and Cambridge, she spent seven years in full-time ministry in rural parishes in the diocese of Ely.

For Jonathan, whom God has truly given.

Also for Elizabeth and Graham,
and for my beloved mother and father,
Bess and Ron Hammond.

Heavenly Father, maker of all things,
you enable us to share in your work of creation.

PASSIONATE
CHRISTIANITY

A journey to the cross

Cally Hammond

First published in Great Britain in 2007

Society for Promoting Christian Knowledge
36 Causton Street
London SW1P 4ST

British Library Cataloguing-in-Publication Data
A catalogue record for this book is available from the British Library

ISBN 978–0–281–05882–2

1 3 5 7 9 10 8 6 4 2

Typeset by Graphicraft Ltd, Hong Kong
Printed in Great Britain by Ashford Colour Press

Produced on paper from sustainable forests

Contents

———◆———

Introduction

To explain what the Passion means is like trying to define an abstract idea like 'goodness'. If the Passion of Jesus Christ could be reduced to a few simple concepts, it could not be deep or rich enough to sustain a living faith, or to do justice to the amazing complexity of human life. Yet if it makes no sense of ordinary human existence, why should anyone choose to put their faith in it, or live their life by it?

In ordinary modern usage, 'passion' means *love*, particularly love expressed in physical terms, or with great intensity. But Christians use the term 'the Passion' in a special sense: to describe what happened to Jesus at the end of his life, at the point when he stopped being a doer (a teacher, preacher, healer and worker of signs and wonders), and became the man to whom things were done. In other words, when he became the object of others' actions, rather than acting himself. In this special sense, the word 'Passion' encompasses suffering, endurance, refusal to retaliate, and also love, expressed in physical form, and with an intensity we can barely grasp.

For some, the focus of their Christian faith is on Jesus the teacher, preacher, healer and worker of signs and wonders. However, it is in his Passion, when he came to the end of his active ministry, and became the one who suffered, that the heart of Christian faith resides. In other words, it is not just what Jesus did that saves us, but what he was, and is, and ever shall be. The events of the Passion take us to the heart of Jesus' very being, and so into the mystery of our salvation.

Introduction

This book began as a series of Lent addresses delivered in Norwich Cathedral in 2006. The addresses were offered as an aid to entering into the Passion, to give purpose and conviction to the Lenten pilgrimage, so renewing our encounter with the Lord in his suffering and redeeming love. It is often helpful to focus on small details when we want to understand a bigger picture, and this is certainly true of the Passion. I found my way into the Passion by means of five traditional meditations, each on a specific episode in Jesus' journey to the cross, known as the 'sorrowful mysteries'. The sorrowful mysteries are part of a prayer known as the rosary. This is traditionally prayed by Roman Catholics as a meditation on the life, death and resurrection of Jesus, but it can also be used by Christians of all denominations as a helpful way of meditating on the Passion.

After praying the sorrowful mysteries regularly for many years I felt sure they could be a door that opened up the meaning of the Passion. I say a door, not a window, because the sorrowful mysteries give us more than a mere view of a distant, unreachable reality. They can help us to journey from one world (that of the everyday) into another – the world of ultimate reality and ultimate meaning. The five sorrowful mysteries can all be found in Mark's Gospel and are:

- the agony in the garden of Gethsemane (Mark 14.32–42);
- the scourging (Mark 14.61–65; 15.1–15);
- the crowning with thorns (Mark 15.16–20);
- the carrying of the cross (Mark 15.21–25);
- the crucifixion (Mark 15.25–39).

When we really focus our attention on these key moments in the Passion, we move into a new realm of encounter; for the Passion is not only a historical event we can read about, but something we can experience, and in which we can participate.

These five events in Jesus' life encourage us to think deeply, both emotionally and intellectually, about the meaning of faith. These two strands, the emotional and the intellectual, we must hold together. For it is fundamental to the Christian faith that human beings are not, as the earliest heretics would have preferred, spirits temporarily and regrettably attached to physical bodies. Instead we are body and soul together, created in God's image. And it is to our whole selves – soul, mind, intellect, body, emotion and feelings – that the Passion must speak.

For two thousand years the Passion story has worked upon human minds, and drawn people to an awareness that Jesus was more than a good man suffering unjustly; in the events of the Passion the truth of God is disclosed. This is not just a message for the converted. It is a beacon of hope, a promise of transformation. So part of this book is about entering into the sorrowful mysteries, to see them from the inside, *imaginatively*; but it will also be imperative to take a step back, and consider them from the outside, *dis-passionately*. That is the best way to see both what the Passion says to people of faith and how, by drawing on the basis of common human experience, it can help us to speak to those outside the faith. For the Passion has to make sense to everyone, not just to Christians. Jesus did not die so that a committed minority could reassure themselves about their ultimate destiny. He died for the sins of the world, the just for the unjust: 'For Christ also suffered for sins once for all, the righteous for the unrighteous, in order to bring you to God' (1 Peter 3.18). The challenge for the Church today is to search for meaning in the death of Jesus, both for Christians and for non-Christians.

It is this sense of the redemption of the world by our Lord Jesus Christ that we have to hold on to, because the Church is not a private club for the righteous few: it is for everyone. The death of Christ is a profound mystery – not something open to glib or slick explanations – and it is something that all of us can grasp and trust in.

This book is arranged in five chapters, to be used either for a group to work through weekly during Lent, or for private study. Each chapter begins with a passage from Mark's Gospel according to the New Revised Standard Version (though other Gospel passages and versions could be used), and with an illustration to aid meditation and prayer. Each concludes with questions for group discussion or further thought, and with a simple prayer.

Obsecration before the crucifix

Lord by this sweet and saving sign,
Defend us from our foes and thine.

Jesus, by thy wounded feet,
Direct our path aright:
Jesus, by thy nailed hands,
Move ours to deeds of love:
Jesus, by thy pierced side,
Cleanse our desires:
Jesus, by thy crown of thorns,
Annihilate our pride:
Jesus, by thy silence,
Shame our complaints:
Jesus, by thy parched lips,
Curb our cruel speech:
Jesus, by thy closing eyes,
Look on our sin no more:
Jesus, by thy broken heart,
Knit ours to thee.

And by this sweet and saving sign,
Lord, draw us to our peace and thine.
Richard Crashaw (1613–49)
and others

1

The agony in the garden

Mark 14.32–42

They went to a place called Gethsemane; and he said to his disciples, 'Sit here while I pray.' He took with him Peter and James and John, and began to be distressed and agitated. And he said to them, 'I am deeply grieved, even to death; remain here, and keep awake.' And going a little farther, he threw himself on the ground and prayed that, if it were possible, the hour might pass from him. He said, 'Abba, Father, for you all things are possible; remove this cup from me; yet, not what I want, but what you want.' He came and found them sleeping; and he said to Peter, 'Simon, are you asleep? Could you not keep awake one hour? Keep awake and pray that you may not come into the time of trial; the spirit indeed is willing, but the flesh is weak.' And again he went away and prayed, saying the same words. And once more he came and found them sleeping, for their eyes were very heavy; and they did not know what to say to him. He came a third time and said to them, 'Are you still sleeping and taking your rest? Enough! The hour has come; the Son of Man is betrayed into the hands of sinners. Get up, let us be going. See, my betrayer is at hand.'

The story of Gethsemane is painful to read. In it, we see Jesus in a moment of mental anguish, encountering his fears. Almost everyone who reads this passage, even for the first time, knows that beyond it lies the crucifixion. So there is a gap between the viewpoint of the characters in the story and those who read it, a gap which is called dramatic irony. Inside the story, the characters do not know what the future holds, but we, the readers, know all too well. One of the funny things about such stories is that this does not make the end boring but quite the reverse – the tension is all the greater. Gethsemane, the first of the sorrowful mysteries, is the beginning of the way of sorrows, the road on which Jesus set his foot after the Last Supper, and which led directly to Calvary. Every year the story is repeated, and every year the torment of Gethsemane speaks to us again.

We can approach this story in many ways. We can ask the historical questions, which help to set the context, and remind us that all this is real history. When did it take place? Who was Pontius Pilate, and Caiaphas? Where did it all happen? We can also ask theological questions about the identity of Jesus. Was he a good man setting us a good example? Was he God 'disguised' as a human? Was his suffering real? Did he have a choice? And of course we can ask spiritual questions. How did his death make a difference to those who loved him? What does the Passion of Jesus mean for us? How can we come to understand it more deeply?

Just like today, in the early Church many things drew people to faith in Jesus. But two stand out: first, the belief that God had become a human being in Jesus; second, the belief that God had raised Jesus from the dead. These two beliefs are cornerstones of our faith, and they are usually referred to as 'the incarnation',* and 'the resurrection'. For a few, such belief

---

* 'Incarnation' means that God himself became a human being, Jesus. The Church has spent centuries working out how this could happen, and what it might mean. The task is ongoing.

came through their personal physical encounter with Jesus before or after his resurrection – or in the case of Peter, the other apostles and Mary Magdalene, both. For others, the encounter was not physical, though it was no less real for that – Paul encountered the risen Lord, and his conversion experience has been repeated in millions of lives since. But the first Christians had a problem: how to speak to a culture which did not share either that experience of encounter, or that belief in incarnation and resurrection. The surrounding pagan culture, to which Paul carried the gospel, regarded resurrection of the body as an insult to the purity of the soul. Worse, it considered the idea of an incarnate God ridiculous. So the first defenders of Christianity, the early Christian apologists, tried to explain their faith in terms which pagans could accept. They were putting into action the principle by which Paul justified his way of preaching to Gentiles: 'I have become all things to all people, that I might by any means save some. I do it all for the sake of the gospel, that I may share in its blessings' (1 Corinthians 9.22).

The Church today goes on proclaiming belief in the incarnation and the resurrection, as it always has done. Those two cornerstones of the faith are as incomprehensible now to those on the 'outside' as they always were; and they are still open to criticism and ridicule. But whereas in the early centuries of Christianity philosophy was a common language both for those attacking the faith and those defending it, nowadays confidence in the reasonableness of Christian faith is more likely to be undermined by the language of science, and the expectation of scientific justification for our beliefs about the material world. As a result, ways of defending Christian faith have split off in different directions. One path is that of fundamentalism, which claims to insist on the literal truth of the Bible and its inerrancy, using (and abusing) the tools of science to defend these presuppositions. Another is the development of a historical, critical and literary approach to the Bible, which assumes that truth (including factual truth) is contained in scripture, but that scripture has no pretensions to *scientific* truth. Of course on one level, such debate need not affect individual believers, who may accept such doctrines as the incarnation and resurrection as they have been taught them, or as they have discovered them, without worrying very much about how they harmonize with competing and apparently contradictory beliefs.

In the ancient world, matter, and the realm of the material, was widely understood to be changeable and corruptible, and therefore inferior, whereas the highest realities were those which were unseen – the spiritual and non-material, things which, because they are lasting, have inherent value. In the modern world, science seems to have done away with the capacity for physical things to have inherent value; the world is no longer good or evil, it simply *is*. Yet the need for a right attitude to the stewardship of creation, and the wise application of science to this end, has never been more pressing: 'one cannot dissociate the plan of creation from the plan of redemption' (Pope Paul VI, 2002, p. 31).

Just like the first Christians, Christians today have to find a way of speaking to the world in terms it can understand; but this is only a starting point from which to explore and accept the incarnation and resurrection for what they eternally are. Once the Church starts to give way to the world's assumption – 'resurrection makes no scientific sense; God-made-flesh is meaningless' – it has lost its way. Today, there is a loss of confidence in the Christian message, even among Christians, because of the pervasive climate of belief that science 'trumps' faith, and makes it meaningless or ridiculous. Some contemporary would-be defenders of the faith water down Christian belief in the incarnation and resurrection, and concentrate on what 'the world' can understand in its own terms. This is not so different from what one early defender of Christianity did. Justin Martyr (died *c*. AD 165) seized upon one fundamental aspect of the Church's understanding of Jesus as the perfect means of linking up pagan and Christian thought. That fundamental aspect was the Christian idea of the divine Word, which in Greek (*Logos*) also means 'reason'. It originates in the Gospel of John (1.1–14), though Justin may not have known the Fourth Gospel directly. The Logos seemed to Justin to bind the pursuit of pagan philosophy and Christian belief together, as if they were built upon the same foundation, and so perfectly compatible. It was an important insight, and it certainly helped the early Church with its task of defining the relationship of Christ to God the Father. But Justin was motivated by a desire to make Christianity seem acceptable, and non-threatening, to the pagan majority, and he certainly underplayed Christian beliefs which would be less appealing and familiar to a pagan reader, such as redemption.

Christians are in danger of doing something similar today, when they reach out to the world in the only terms they think it will understand, by presenting the faith as a bulwark against immorality. This implies that the Church goes along with secular assumptions that faith is about morality, that its purpose is to make people behave, and to control the innate human tendency to wrongdoing. In reality, as a Christian friend once said to me, Christianity has nothing whatever to do with *being good*. It has everything to do with faith, hope, and love directed towards the creator, the redeemer, the sustainer God. Moral goodness is a lovely, blessed *by-product* of faith; but it is not the end, or the purpose, or the heart of faith.

Understanding the Passion must begin with the cornerstones of faith. But in discussing the incarnation and the resurrection, something has been left out. So far, I have only mentioned two cornerstones, but the temple of our faith has three. As well as the incarnation and the resurrection, we must also rest the edifice of our faith upon the *atonement*. Incarnation speaks to us of God entering into the reality of human existence. Resurrection speaks to us of God giving us hope that our existence (and our relationship with him) is rooted in eternity. Atonement speaks to us of the mystery of the cross, by which God and sinners have been reconciled. Of these three cornerstones, only 'resurrection' is a biblical word (in Greek, *anastasis*). 'Incarnation' (Greek *enanthropesis*) was used by the early Church to encapsulate the meaning of John 1.14, 'the word became flesh' – it points to the act of God becoming human. 'Atonement' is more complicated. The language of atonement and atoning sacrifices is found in the Old Testament, but the only (possible) instance in the New Testament is at Romans 5.11, where modern translations now render the Greek word (*katallage*) as 'reconciliation'. 'Atonement' is best avoided in translating this verse, because when theologians use it, they can take it to mean not only reconciliation but also propitiation (the turning aside of God's anger) and expiation (cleansing from guilt or ritual pollution).

The faith to believe that Jesus is the incarnate Son of God is a gift. We can try and understand the incarnation in terms which make philosophical and/or theological sense, or we can simply accept our belief as the gift it truly is. We can believe that Jesus rose from the dead, however we manage to understand that. I have worked my way round from a sceptical position to one of absolute confidence in the incarnation and the resurrection, though it is interesting to reflect that my doubts about the physical, historical truth of those cornerstones of faith did not undermine my faith in God or Jesus. Perhaps that is a hopeful sign for those who possess greater scientific expertise than I do, and so must wrestle harder with scientific challenges to faith. One thing is clear: conviction and peace in faith do not come to us through intellectual endeavour, but through the gift of God; and we can only hope that others will find them too, through the Holy Spirit's guidance.

With the third cornerstone, the atonement, the problem of understanding is at least as great as it is for the incarnation or the resurrection. It is the hardest, most mysterious thing in all the Christian faith. The most difficult question children always asked me when I was a parish priest was 'Why did Jesus have to die?' The way that this question is phrased shows that one of Christianity's first lessons has been absorbed – that in some sense, Jesus' death was *inevitable*. The words 'have to die' could suggest to us that Jesus was *fated* or *destined* to die. This is the wrong way to understand it. Jesus did not have to die in the sense that his death was *predestined*. God did not decide that this was how everything was going to work out, and programme Jesus like a robot to do what God wanted. Jesus was not made to die, nor forced to die. But it came to pass that his being killed was inevitable. It certainly seemed so to him. It is interesting to ask at what point death became, for Jesus, the unavoidable end of his actions. There is a moment described by Luke, in which – memorable phrase – he 'turned his face to Jerusalem' (9.51). This echoes the calling of the prophet Ezekiel: 'The word of the LORD came to me: Son of man, set your face toward Jerusalem and preach against the sanctuaries; prophesy against the land of Israel' (Ezekiel 21.1–2). The implication of this echo is that, just like Ezekiel, Jesus will meet hostility and physical threat because of everything that he did and said in obedience to God. Jesus knew how God's people had persecuted the prophets who prophesied against them. He must also have known that, by acting as the prophets before him had done, he would infuriate the religious and secular authorities and perhaps forfeit his life.

The children's question 'Why did Jesus have to die?' goes directly to the very heart of the Passion. Yet no answer that I gave could ever meet their need to understand, because the Passion of Jesus is not really something we can finally make sense of verbally. The children learned the meaning through attending to the story, and so should we. Yet the question also carries with it another: 'What does Jesus' death *mean* for us?' Everyone who thinks about Christian faith must face these questions, and, if they do not find clear and simple answers, must at least find a way to live with their inability to put deep spiritual convictions into words. After all, Jesus the Word became flesh, a human being, precisely because God knows that we understand as much through relationships and personal encounters as we do through intellectual argument.

So one reason for exploring the Passion is to make sense of it to ourselves; the other is so that we can make better sense of it to others. This journey can be a sobering one; it may be painful as well, but it is truly a way of entering into the Passion, and so uniting ourselves with Christ. I have already hinted that I think reason, logic, science and study can only help us so far. There comes a point at which reason and understanding (the attempt to grasp intellectually the meaning of the Passion) have to merge into something else, as we enter in prayer, in imagination and in meditation into the reality of the Passion. This is not said out of hostility to reason as a means of access to the divine. When we understand it properly, reason is one of the ways in which God discloses himself, and is an attribute of his nature. There is a long history of Christianity rejecting reason in order to make way for faith, and an almost equally long tradition of Christians insisting that faith and understanding have to go together. Augustine put it as a paradox: 'Do you wish to understand? Then believe. For God has said by his prophet, "Unless you believe, you will not understand." So do not seek to understand so that you may believe; rather believe, so that you may understand' (*Tractate on John's Gospel* 29.6, quoting Isaiah 7.9). Sometimes it can be helpful to set aside our human instinct for analysis, and make room for other facets of our mental and spiritual awareness, to help us to a better understanding of the atonement, without which the Passion of Jesus remains as opaque and mysterious as ever.

The journey to the cross begins with Jesus at the point where he makes a terrible, terrifying decision: in the garden of Gethsemane. What happens in that time of prayer is not a sudden decision, but the fruit of long reflection and preparation. We can see this from the context in which the Passion is set; and here it is helpful to look back at the earlier part of Mark 14. A woman came to anoint Jesus with costly ointment. He revealed the meaning of her action: 'She has done what she could; she has anointed my body beforehand *for its burial*' (Mark 14.8). This was the turning point in the drama of the Passion: immediately afterwards, Judas went out to plot with the chief priests how to hand Jesus over. Once his body was anointed for burial, Jesus prepared to eat the Passover with his disciples – the last meal they would share together. He broke bread, and gave them the broken fragments, with the words 'this is my body'. He gave them wine, with the words 'this is my blood, shed for many'. For the Jewish food laws, avoiding the eating of blood was of supreme importance. Knowing this clarifies how extraordinary Jesus' words at the Last Supper really were: 'You shall not eat the blood of any creature, for the life of every creature is its blood' (Leviticus 17.14) becomes: 'This

is my blood of the covenant, which is poured out for many'
(Mark 14.24).

We should not forget how shocking this commandment
must have been. There could be no mistaking the profound
significance of what was taking place. The Gospel record is clear:
Jesus foresaw his death, he knew what was about to happen.
He knew his body would be broken, and that his blood would
be shed. He also made it plain, in what he said over the cup,
that his death was to be an event with far-reaching consequences. The disciples understood the significance of that Last
Supper too – slow to understand as they so often were, here
they did grasp his meaning. They all promised to follow him,
even to death. Not just Peter but all of them made that promise. Then, when Jesus was in the garden of Gethsemane,
'Distress and anguish overwhelmed him, and he said to them,
"My heart is ready to break with grief. Stop here, and stay
awake with me"' (Matthew 26.37–38, Revised English Bible).
Death was in the air that night. Jesus saw it coming. So did
those who loved and followed him. And he also saw that he
had a choice. In his prayer in the garden, he was tormented by
the possibility that things could have been otherwise.

One of my favourite writers has said that the keenest of all
anguish is self-reproach; but surely the sharpest of all griefs is
knowing that *it could all have been different.* This is the essence
of Jesus' grief in the garden – that it could all have been different. He could have chosen a simple, happy life, fulfilled by
ordinary human companionship and the love which is most
creative, the love which brings new life into the world. It is clear
that Jesus loved children. He set them before us as examples of
how we are to live, and to approach God. He could have been
like everyone else – and what a powerful longing and temptation that can be. A married man with a family, children to delight

in and watch growing up. A future. Peace. Solitude, which he often longed for but rarely secured.

I said earlier that the five sorrowful mysteries are traditionally a form of meditation. This form of meditation is a kind of prayer in which, in our imagination, we enter into the Bible story and become part of it. We can do this by imagining how the agony in the garden unfolded, and how it felt. Stepping into the scene, perhaps as one of the disciples, perhaps viewing things from a hidden vantage point in the garden, or as part of the scenery, we find that the story comes to life in our imagination. This meditative process works in two ways. It is partly about us entering into the sufferings of Jesus, and partly about us recognizing him in our own sorrows, our own Gethsemanes. Everyone has had the experience of facing a difficult decision, a decision which would cause pain whatever choice was made, whatever course of action was adopted. It might not be momentous in the eyes of others, but that is not what matters. The impossibility of choosing a desirable outcome – that is the essence of the pain. This is the real meaning behind the word 'tragic' (which is so often misapplied and cheapened): that there is no desirable outcome to be found; that there can be no pain-free resolution of a dilemma.

Even in the garden of Gethsemane, Jesus was still free to choose. He could have walked away: he could have left Jerusalem secretly, headed back to Nazareth, and settled down. That might seem a relatively easy choice. But with that choice another kind of pain would have come: the torment of *knowing what is right, but denying it.* If we have known the agony of an insoluble dilemma, when every choice would bring pain, here too we find common ground with Jesus. All of us experience temptations to deny what is right, out of fear of the consequences of sticking to what Jesus called the narrow way

(Matthew 7.13). All of us have given in to that temptation, perhaps by making a decision which was easier or more pleasant
for us, while knowing that there was another, harder path to
follow, and that through cowardice we rejected it. Perhaps we
chose to keep silent when we should have spoken out, from fear
of ridicule, or reluctance to stand out from the crowd. Perhaps
that harder choice, that narrow way, was only apparent to us,
and unnoticed by others. But we cannot hide our failures from
our own consciences.

Again, each one of us knows best the ways in which we have
failed in our calling by knowing what is right yet denying it.
We know that our silence can be as much a betrayal as any
words spoken in deceit. We may have been enjoying the com-
pany of friends when one of them caught us utterly unprepared
by telling a racist joke; or they may have said something in a
moment of casual prejudice, against which any Christian ought
to raise a voice of protest. And we were afraid to speak out. This
denial of right can even happen through our polite reluctance
to embarrass others or appear to criticize them. When someone takes the name of Jesus Christ in vain and uses it as a swear
word, it seems so much uglier and more horrible to use the name
of him who died upon the cross as an expression of anger or
disgust than to use any of the non-blasphemous swear words.
But when people do so, do we dare to ask them not to, or are
we too afraid of sounding 'holier than thou'? At moments like
this, our sense of shame is very much bound up in knowing
what is right, but denying it.

For Jesus himself, and for anyone who reads this part of
the Gospel knowing what is to follow later, Gethsemane is a
moment of vision into the future. It is the moment at which
Jesus looks forward to see his own death. How much he was
able to anticipate, or how clearly he saw into the unfolding of
the Passion, it is impossible to say. The death he foresaw in

the garden is so familiar in all its details that it can be difficult to come to grips with its wider significance. But in the first instance, like every death, it is something to be understood by the individual facing it, rather than any social or family group. It goes without saying that not all deaths are the same. Some are quick, painless, welcomed, even beautiful; others shocking, agonizing, dreaded or prolonged. Did Jesus know what *kind* of death he faced? It is hard to tell. He knew on what grounds the religious authorities would want him condemned – blasphemy. And he knew on what grounds the Roman authorities mistrusted him – he seemed to them an insurgent. So the likelihood was, unless he fled and hid, either stoning or crucifixion. Either way, his death would be unimaginably horrible. What did this do to Jesus the man, in his agony in the garden?

Our own experience once more gives us a glimpse into his mind. When we have to face physical pain, the fear of it can consume our thinking. We ask ourselves how we will cope; we worry about what will happen if we break down, anxious lest our failure to withstand pain may be seen as weakness or cowardice. Jesus' thinking in Gethsemane cannot have been entirely different from what our own might be if we were facing the virtual certainty of painful and humiliating death. No wonder Jesus' heart was ready to break with grief. That would be the ordinary human reaction. Jesus, like all of us, might fear to die in pain, hated and abused. But there is another dimension to his dying – a cosmic dimension.* This cosmic dimension makes for a deeper, more dreadful kind of grief. So he went to his sleepy disciples, and said to them: 'Could you not keep awake one hour? Keep awake and pray that you may

---

* This will become clearer in the final chapter, on the crucifixion itself.

not come into the time of trial; the spirit indeed is willing, but the flesh is weak' (Mark 14.37–38).

When he said that, he was not only speaking to them, but to himself as well – 'the spirit indeed is willing, but the flesh is weak'. We are reminded that Jesus was not simply God in human dress, with the appearance of a man but the reality of all-powerful divinity. No. He was truly human, vulnerable to pain, suffering and uncertainty, as all of us are. This is what the incarnation really means – that God could not have saved us except by becoming truly and completely like us.

We read in the prologue of John's Gospel that 'the Word became flesh and lived among us' (John 1.14). But here, in the garden of Gethsemane, the reality, and the ultimate significance, of those words first truly hits home. For us, as for the first followers of Jesus, as for all the millions of people in the centuries in between, death is the great enemy, the destroyer – the unknown for which we cannot practise, cannot really prepare ourselves, which we have no control over, and which we cannot imagine. And in Gethsemane, God, in Jesus, enters into the mystery of human agony in the face of death. I am not just talking now about our own death. I am also thinking of the loss of those we love. There is the agony of every parent who has lost a child. The sorrow of every child for whom the world seems bitter, cold and empty when their mother or father is dead. The grief of everyone who has found that a friend they cared for would rather commit suicide than live another day – and they had not even noticed. The torment of a family riven by a feud whose origins are long forgotten, but whose grudges are nurtured and fomented, until the last chance of reconciliation is snatched away by death, unleashing floods of recrimination and guilt. And there is the loss of friends and family that increases in speed and number as our own years on earth increase – urging us, almost forcing us, to reflect on the meaning of death. Funerals become all too common, too regular a part of the turning of the seasons, the passing of the years.

When someone is close to death, relatives find themselves in a bizarre kind of limbo – a world in which they cannot plan for the future – because, in that limbo, 'the future' has no meaning. They cannot book their holidays, look forward to their birthdays, make arrangements for Christmas. This is a world in which they do not know whether they should go home and take a bath; put the washing on; watch a programme on the telly. The hours and minutes they once enjoyed without noticing, simply because their value was not to be counted, become impossible to tolerate once their number becomes finite. There is even a sense of anger, frustration, guilt, that they are trapped in a torment of uncertainty. No wonder that we often describe death as a blessed release – it can be so not just for the person who dies, but for everyone who loves that person too.

What Jesus seems to be looking for in the garden of Gethsemane is an end to this agonizing uncertainty; an end to might-have-beens; an end to the possibility that he could choose otherwise. He may have known all his adult life that death in shame and dishonour would be his end; but that was not the same as actually facing it, right now, immediately at hand. Every one of us, being human, knows that we will one day die. But until we know how and when – if we ever do know that – our minds cannot begin to deal with the agony of letting go of life. If the first sorrowful mystery, Gethsemane, teaches us anything about the meaning of Jesus' death, it must be that he has shared in our limbo of uncertainty; shared in the torment of might-have-beens, of 'if only'; that he has shared in the death of hope, and the ending of all dreams, for an ordinary human future.

Every year we watch the drama of the Passion unfold; and we could conceivably do so as the gods in the ancient poems of Homer or Virgil watched human suffering – at a distance, detached, untouched by all the pain. But we can, and should, choose to do more than this – because in the Passion story we should not be *spectators* but *participants*. Meditating on the sorrowful mysteries, exploring the themes of the Passion, helps to make it real to us, so that we can enter into the sufferings of Jesus our brother, and learn to walk with him the way of the cross. Jesus in the Gospel story, in his humanity, cannot tell the future; but we know it, because every time we enter into the drama of Holy Week we do so as people who have already made the paschal mystery of Easter our own. The task now, through the first sorrowful mystery, is to imagine that moment of the agony in the garden as if for the first time, just as Jesus once had to face it: without the comfort of Easter around the corner, without the vindication of resurrection, and exaltation to glory.

What does the first of the sorrowful mysteries show us now, as we gather at the start of Lent to journey with Jesus? It shows how we can turn our face to the cross, and resolutely accept that our way as Christians lies in that direction. Somehow we can, we must, find the courage to enter into the agony in the garden, and to be ready to leave Gethsemane to face whatever may come, trusting – even in the midst of grief and anguish – as Jesus trusted and prayed that night: 'Abba,* Father, for you all things are possible; remove this cup from me; yet, not what I want, but what you want' (Mark 14.36).

---

* 'Abba' is the Aramaic word for father. Aramaic was Jesus' mother tongue.

Questions for further thought and discussion

1 How do you prepare for the unfolding of the Passion at the end of Lent, either in church or as an individual?

2 Did Jesus have any real choice to make in Gethsemane?

3 Is it true that Christianity has nothing to do with being good?

4 Do you think that studying the Passion story in detail will deepen your faith, or weaken it?

A prayer for the mystery of the agony in the garden

God our Father,
help me to understand the agony of Jesus my Lord.
In my difficult decisions and hard choices,
may I be united with him,
and so grow in compassion and holiness,
through the same Jesus Christ our Lord. Amen.

2

The scourging of Jesus

Mark 14.61–65; 15.1–15

The high priest asked Jesus, 'Are you the Messiah, the Son of the Blessed One?' Jesus said, 'I am; and "you will see the Son of Man seated at the right hand of the Power", and "coming with the clouds of heaven."' Then the high priest tore his clothes and said, 'Why do we still need witnesses? You have heard his blasphemy! What is your decision?' All of them condemned him as deserving death. Some began to spit on him, to blindfold him, and to strike him, saying to him, 'Prophesy!' The guards also took him over and beat him. . . .

As soon as it was morning, the chief priests held a consultation with the elders and scribes and the whole council. They bound Jesus, led him away, and handed him over to Pilate. Pilate asked him, 'Are you the King of the Jews?' He answered him, 'You say so.' Then the chief priests accused him of many things. Pilate asked him again, 'Have you no answer? See how many charges they bring against you.' But Jesus made no further reply, so that Pilate was amazed.

Now at the festival he used to release a prisoner for them, anyone for whom they asked. Now a man called Barabbas was in prison with the rebels who had committed murder during the insurrection. So the crowd came and began to ask Pilate to do for them according to his custom. Then he answered them, 'Do you want me to release for you the King of the Jews?' For he realized that it was out of jealousy that the chief priests had handed him over. But the chief priests stirred up the crowd to have him release Barabbas for them instead. Pilate spoke to them again, 'Then what do you wish me to do with the man you call the King of the Jews?' They shouted back, 'Crucify him!' Pilate asked them, 'Why, what evil has he done?' But they shouted all the more, 'Crucify him!' So Pilate, wishing to satisfy the crowd, released Barabbas for them; and after flogging Jesus, he handed him over to be crucified.

In the garden of Gethsemane, we saw how Jesus moved from indecision to resolution: from the last hope that things could be otherwise and that he could choose to continue his earthly life, to the acceptance that events would have to run their course. It is becoming clear that to grasp the meaning of the Passion we have to move out of the role of spectators, and into that of participants. So we turn to the second sorrowful mystery, the scourging of Jesus. Like Gethsemane, it can be very painful to think about, because it forces us to contemplate our Lord and Saviour enduring dreadful physical punishment. There is a danger that the still greater horror which lies ahead for Jesus will obscure the severity of what he must endure now. But as soon as we start to meditate on the scene, that danger is averted. Our generation has become more sensitive than ever before in human history to the need to protect the integrity and worth of the whole human person. We have begun, however clumsily, to try and give effective legal protection for every person against the threat or reality of humiliating physical punishment. In practice, such protection is confined to those living in developed societies with financial and legal safeguards against cruelty or exploitation – and even there it is far from universally secure – but the principle is a sound one. In the light of this, the scourging of Jesus, however painful, has its own distinctive lesson to teach us about the meaning of the Passion, and its own message for us in our day.

The scourging of Jesus is one stage in the unjust judicial process by which he is condemned. In John's version of the Passion, Pilate asks Jesus a very reasonable question: 'What have you done?' (John 18.35). And twice his words to the crowd reinforce this impression of reasonableness: 'I find no case against him' (18.38; 19.4). Pilate's voice of reason, however, is drowned out by a host of clamouring voices denouncing Jesus as a danger to established religion and established government. What confronts us now is a conflict between the conscience of the individual and the demands of the common good. It is the inevitable result of the clash between one man's beliefs, words and actions, and the established view of what is right.

We have already seen that Jesus probably knew, from quite early in his ministry, that his actions would lead to his persecution by the religious authorities. Jesus knew that the coming of the Son of Man would cause resentment and hostility. Jesus also knew that most of us have a streak of hardened selfishness in us, and that most of us are quite uncomfortable with real goodness because it throws our own selfishness into too sharp relief. This unpleasant fact about human nature is underlined by one of his most disturbing parables: the workers in the vineyard (Matthew 20.1–16). A householder hires labourers for his vineyard, and then later hires more. Those who come last are paid the same as those who have worked from the beginning, who have borne the heat and burden of the day. The workers who have been hard at it all day object. Notice the form their objection takes: 'These last worked only one hour, *and you have made them equal to us.*' They are resentful that there are to be no gradations in status, according to how long each has worked in the householder's service.

When I first read this parable, I saw it as a parable of the Church. To me, the grumbling workers were like regular churchgoers who thought they deserved preferential treatment and a long-service bonus; who resented newcomers and tried to make them as unwelcome as possible. The householder was God, whose generosity, unlike that of the people hired first, was boundless and overflowing. Perhaps this says as much about me, and my low expectations of Christian welcome, as it does about the meaning of the parable. But we should consider first how Jesus originally meant it, and what its particular point was for his hearers. It comes just after the story of a rich young man (Matthew 19.16–30): everyone is astonished to find that Jesus does not commend him by saying that his riches are a proof of God's favour. Peter was so astonished that he spoke out and challenged Jesus: 'Look, we have left everything and followed you. What then will we have?' There is a very serious challenge embedded in that Gospel account. Surely every Christian can recognize themselves in the asking of this question. Even if the words have never been spoken, the assumption is there. It is a deep-seated and natural human instinct to look for a *quid pro quo*, and we are only human. 'Look, we have left everything and followed you. What then will we have?'

The parable of the workers in the vineyard is Jesus' answer to that question. There is no first-class treatment in the kingdom of heaven: no reserved seats, no privileged membership, no platinum card. Each person makes the same covenant with God – faithfulness is demanded of both sides. The reward for each person is the agreed one – as settled at the making of the covenant. Yet why should newcomers be greeted on seemingly more favourable terms? Isn't this inherently unfair, just as when mobile phone companies offer better deals to new customers than to the customers they have already?

That parallel betrays a fundamental weakness in our understanding of God. It is highly significant that the parable speaks as truly and accurately to the Church today as it did to the Jews of Jesus' time. There is no Office of Fair Trading in heaven – no place to complain to when the new customers get the same reward for less work. And the only sensible conclusion we can draw from that fact is that our relationship with God is not a bargain or contract. It is not the case that we agree to carry out certain functions – be good, keep God's law, worship him – and then God rewards us for keeping our side of the bargain. He makes exactly the same deal with each person; time is of no consequence, because God is not interested in how many things we have done for him, or how long we have been doing them. He is only interested in our inner disposition to love him and respond to him. Again, goodness, and good deeds, are a lovely by-product of faith in God. They do not earn God's love for us, nor do they prove our love for God. Think about what the workers' complaint of unfair treatment is *really* saying: 'We don't regard serving you as a privilege and a joy but as a boring, tedious chore.' To be part of God's family is meant to be a joy, not a bore.

The householder's answer to the labourers is God's answer to the Jewish people, who expected preferential treatment compared to other nations. It is also God's answer to Christians who treat the Church as a club of which they are charter-members, and where others are welcomed only on their terms, in a strict pecking order. To come down to what is entirely familiar from everyday experience, it is the answer of every sensible parent to squabbling children who complain that one sibling is being favoured unfairly. Love is not to be measured by goods and services; it knows no limit of time or place. It is, as Paul taught, the greatest of the three things which last for ever. And the very fact that it is eternal means that it cannot be subject to everyday human rules.

If we look at matters in this light, if we remember the re-action of those workers in the vineyard, the reaction of the religious and imperial authorities to Jesus becomes easier to understand. The radical teaching of Jesus was that God's love cuts across our ordinary human understanding of earning or deserving. That was never going to go down well with those in authority. *Quid pro quo* is not only a deep-seated religious instinct, but also a great reciprocal principle of human co-existence: 'You scratch my back and I'll scratch yours.' Jesus utterly rejects that view:

> You have heard that it was said, 'An eye for an eye and a tooth for a tooth.' But I say to you, Do not resist an evildoer. But if anyone strikes you on the right cheek, turn the other also; and if anyone wants to sue you and take your coat, give your cloak as well; and if anyone forces you to go one mile, go also the second mile. Give to everyone who begs from you, and do not refuse anyone who wants to borrow from you.
>
> You have heard that it was said, 'You shall love your neigh-bour and hate your enemy.' But I say to you, Love your enemies and pray for those who persecute you, so that you may be children of your Father in heaven; for he makes his sun rise on the evil and on the good, and sends rain on the righteous and on the unrighteous. For if you love those who love you, what reward do you have? Do not even the tax-collectors do the same? And if you greet only your brothers and sisters, what more are you doing than others? Do not even the Gentiles do the same? Be perfect, therefore, as your heavenly Father is perfect.
>
> (Matthew 5.38–48)

Here is a radical new ethic for human society; one which is every bit as outrageous, and counter-cultural, and counter-

intuitive, today as it was then. The law of Moses had expressed
a form of justice with perfect clarity and universal appeal: 'If
any harm follows, then you shall give life for life, eye for eye,
tooth for tooth, hand for hand, foot for foot, burn for burn,
wound for wound, stripe for stripe' (Exodus 21.23–25). This is
called the *lex talionis*, or law of direct retribution. According
to it, the job of human law is to restore balance, to preserve
the status quo. The job of human law is also to act fairly and
proportionately, to maintain an equality of suffering or dis-
advantage. To know that the harm we inflict will be the harm
we suffer teaches us to refrain from inflicting harm – that must
be the logic. Jesus teaches something different. The demands
of his teaching are so extreme that even most Christians re-
sort to reinterpreting them, or just ignore them altogether. He
insists that those who love God must go beyond *lex talionis*
by letting go of wrongs done, and by being willing to endure
wrongs: 'Love your enemies and pray for those who persecute
you, so that you may be children of your Father in heaven.' There
is no reason in this but the inexorable logic of being loving,
forgiving children of a loving, forgiving Father. This imperative
of forgiveness finds its highest expression in the Lord's Prayer –
'Forgive us our trespasses, as we forgive them that trespass
against us.' Not, you will notice, with the *lex talionis* addendum
which Paul threw in, unable to help himself: 'If your enemies
are hungry, feed them; if they are thirsty, give them something
to drink; for by doing this you will heap burning coals on their
heads. Do not be overcome by evil, but overcome evil with
good' (Romans 12.20–21). Here Paul seems to have missed the
point completely – unless, like the good preacher that he is,
he knows that he must start with what people are capable of
hearing and responding to. After all, forgiving people, even for
reasons less than perfect, is still forgiving. Elsewhere Paul (or
some of his followers) seems to show a better understanding of

Jesus' teaching, saying: 'Forgive one another as God in Christ forgave you' (Ephesians 4.32), and 'Forgive each other: as the Lord has forgiven you, so you also must forgive' (Colossians 3.13).

There are three things worth noticing here about forgiveness. First, of all the petitions of the Lord's Prayer, only the prayer to forgive is repeated and explained: 'For if you forgive others their trespasses, your heavenly Father will also forgive you; but if you do not forgive others, neither will your Father forgive your trespasses' (Matthew 6.14). Second, forgiveness gets a whole parable devoted to it at the end of Matthew 18 (the king settling accounts with his slaves). And third (this is an observation from my ministry), of all the topics on which I have preached over the years, the one which has consistently caused the strongest reaction is forgiveness. Every time I have referred in a sermon to the Christian duty to forgive, someone has come up to me after the service and said, 'I felt that sermon was speaking to *me*'. Clearly, there is a good reason why forgiveness is at the heart of Jesus' teaching. He knew, in his wisdom, how many of us carry around secret burdens of resentment, anger, hostility and grudges. He knew too that such things are not good for us, because they damage us as people, they corrupt us, and ultimately they can even destroy us.

Discussing forgiveness may seem to be a distraction from thinking about the scourging of Christ, but we cannot understand the scourging without thinking first of how deeply and intimately Jesus, being human, understood our human nature. Only because of his complete humanity, his incarnation, could he challenge us to move beyond our instinctive desire for revenge, resentment and grudge-bearing. Jesus knew there would be an adverse reaction to his preaching, and to his very way of life, his way of being. There is no challenger of the status quo who does not know likewise. And we who prefer a quiet life, and would rather not get into trouble with the authorities; we who fear conflict and avoid it at any cost, would do well to remember the example of Jesus the next time we are too quick to judge others who campaign vociferously to overturn the status quo on behalf of the oppressed and the voiceless. Just as some who offer hospitality to strangers are entertaining angels unawares (Hebrews 13.2), so some who outrage public opinion and disturb the peace are doing the work of God, and standing in the place of Christ. No doubt they are imperfect imitators of our perfect Lord. But imitators they are.

Mark gives us the simplest version of the trials of Jesus before the Jewish religious authorities and the Roman imperial authorities. Jesus was first taken to the Jewish authorities, but they were not allowed to impose the death penalty. So he was transferred to Pontius Pilate, the Roman governor. Pilate tried to have Jesus freed, recognizing his innocence. He offered the people a get-out clause – he would release Jesus in honour of their festival.

Remember, these were the people who, just days before, in the event we now commemorate on Palm Sunday, had hailed him with hosannas as the successor to King David (Mark 11.10). But the people rejected Jesus, and instead chose Barabbas. Maybe the crowd felt cheated by Jesus. They had welcomed him with cries of victory, hoping that the Messiah would be a mighty warrior who would expel the Romans from their land. When they saw what Jesus really was, they rejected him. It is at least possible that Judas Iscariot was among them – that he too was hoping for a strong rebel leader, and when he realized Jesus had no intention of starting a war, he rejected him. Barabbas, on the other hand, was a leader of armed rebellion against the Romans, and the people loved him for it, and chose him over Jesus. And so at last Pilate, wishing to satisfy the crowd, released Barabbas for them and ordered that Jesus be flogged and then crucified.

When Mel Gibson's film *The Passion of the Christ* was released, one of the things which gave it such an impact was its
super-realistic depiction of some of the events described in
the Gospels. In the long horror of that extraordinary film, one
of the most appalling moments was the scourging of Jesus.
The Roman soldiers who flogged Christ were not portrayed as
military men getting on with an unpleasant but routine duty.
They were shown as vicious, even bestial, in their savagery.
Gibson's Christ fell as he was being flogged, then staggered
back to his feet like the macho hero of an action thriller, prov-
ing his courage and stamina against the cowardly oppressor.
The crudity of this depiction of Jesus was bad enough; but as
a whole the scene was not just cruel, it was demonic. Doubt-
less Gibson had his reasons for it all, according to his own inter-
pretation of the Gospel, but to me, it was a parody of evil. The
sadism of those soldiers reflected a vision of evil which we find
it extremely easy – dangerously easy – to distance ourselves
from, and think, 'I could never be like that'.

History has not recorded for us the inner motivations of those
nameless soldiers. Certainly armies are tough, the Roman army
more so than most. The Romans perfected some of the most
monstrous punishments known to humankind. Decimation
(the execution of every tenth man) was one. Crucifixion was
another. It is possible that the soldiers who punished Jesus were
sadists, who enjoyed inflicting pain. Armies do attract such
people, though the men will often not follow them. Soldiers
are not stupid; they prefer better leaders, and strength alone
is never enough, certainly cruelty is not. Perhaps those soldiers who scourged Jesus relished their job. But it is much
more likely that for them the scourging had none of the
significance we attach to it.

The reality is that evil, especially the infliction of undeserved
pain and suffering, is often humdrum and mundane. It is often

enforced and reinforced in the petty spitefulness of ordinary living: in the refusal, in which we are all complicit, to recognize our own responsibility for the happiness of others; in the ease with which we can justify the sufferings of others as being somehow their own fault. For, after all, if *we* were in their position, we would never drop our moral and personal standards, we would somehow triumph over adversity, because we are . . . well, us. We matter, and they do not.

The Romans crucified Jesus because of the fear that he would lead a rebellion against them, and Pilate gave in, out of fear of seeming too lenient:

> From then on Pilate tried to release him, but the Jews cried out, 'If you release this man, you are no friend of the emperor. Everyone who claims to be a king sets himself against the emperor.'
>
> When Pilate heard these words, he brought Jesus outside and sat on the judge's bench at a place called The Stone Pavement, or in Hebrew Gabbatha. Now it was the day of Preparation for the Passover; and it was about noon. He said to the Jews, 'Here is your King!' They cried out, 'Away with him! Away with him! Crucify him!' Pilate asked them, 'Shall I crucify your King?' The chief priests answered, 'We have no king but the emperor.' Then he handed him over to them to be crucified.
>
> (John 19.12–16)

The keynote in this escalation of violence is fear. Fear of rebellion; fear of punishment; fear of an end to the status quo. Fear makes people turn aside from what they know to be right; it makes them complicit in cruelty and horror. So one real horror of the scourging of Jesus is that Pilate ordered it knowing it was wrong. He justified it to himself as a small evil perpetrated to avoid a greater one – namely a rebellion in the city. We take it almost for granted nowadays that the needs of the majority must prevail, and that if a few people suffer for the good of the majority, it is a price worth paying for a quiet life. This is why during the Second World War innocent people, for instance Germans in the UK and Japanese in the United States, were interned, 'just in case' they presented a threat to wider society. The scourging stands, then, for every trivial injustice (and perhaps some greater ones) in which we have ever been complicit out of laziness or lack of compassion.

Another real horror of the scourging of Jesus is that the soldiers carried it out as a matter of ordinary routine, because, in that phrase made notorious by Nuremberg, they were 'only following orders'. One of the most famous experiments in social psychology ever conducted has a clear relevance to the scourging. It is known as the Milgram experiment, and began in 1961, a year after the trial of the Nazi war criminal Adolf Eichmann in Jerusalem. Stanley Milgram was a psychologist at Yale University who conducted a series of experiments from 1961 to 1963.*

Milgram wanted to find out why Eichmann and his fellow-Nazis in the Holocaust did what they did, and whether they could be regarded as accomplices. Participants in his research were told that they were being asked to take part in a study of memory, though in fact they were being observed to see how easily they would obey persons in authority when ordered to do something which conflicted with what their conscience told them was right. The ostensible question at issue was the role of punishment in teaching. The participants were to be 'teachers', and had to press buttons inflicting a gradually increasing electric shock (ranging from 15 to 450 volts) for every wrong answer their 'learner' gave. It was made clear to the 'teachers' that the level of shock went from 'Slight' to 'Danger: Severe'. In fact the 'learners' were actors, and the electric shocks

---

* The results were published in 1974 as *Obedience to Authority: An Experimental View*, still in print.

were not real. As the supposed voltage was gradually increased to dangerous and extremely painful levels, the reactions of the 'teachers' were monitored. How uncomfortable would they be electrocuting people for wrong answers, just because someone told them to? If they expressed concern about or objections to inflicting such pain, they were given the following responses in this order:

1 Please continue.
2 The experiment requires you to continue, please go on.
3 It is essential that you continue.
4 You have no choice, you must continue.

If the subject still wished to stop after these four responses had been given, the experiment was halted. Otherwise, it was allowed to continue until the subject had given the maximum 450-volt shock three times. This, if real, could be fatal.

Milgram found that more than 60 per cent of participants were willing to inflict fatal voltages. They might protest or question, but most still went ahead and obeyed authority, even though the 'learners' followed instructions to act out the pain their punishment would have caused, by pleading, screaming, begging the teacher to stop, and so on. His experiments have been repeated more than once, but that proportion of compliance in inflicting pain – nearly two-thirds – remains fairly constant. The frightening conclusion of the Milgram experiment was that many people's sense of morality and ordinary human compassion are almost completely overridden by the sense of obligation to do as they are told by an authority figure. It was probably *fear* – fear of incurring anger, criticism or disapproval – which drove people into inflicting inexcusable levels of pain. Milgram observed that 'with numbing regularity good people were seen to knuckle under to the demands of authority and perform actions that were callous and severe. Men who are in everyday life responsible and decent were seduced by the trappings of authority, by the control of their perceptions, and by the uncritical acceptance of the experimenter's definition of the situation into performing harsh acts' (Milgram, 1997, p. 141). From this he concluded that something more dangerous than aggression had been revealed, namely 'the capacity for man to abandon his humanity, indeed the inevitability that he does so, as he merges his unique personality into larger institutional structures (p. 205).

So it is perhaps more depressing than surprising that in the Gospel accounts of the Passion, Pilate stifled his conscience and abandoned his humanity, submerging it beneath the authority and institutions of the Roman Empire. As for the chief priests, when they claimed they had no king but Caesar, they thought they were defending their Law against a trouble-maker, but as Milgram wrote of his subjects, 'once having acted against the victim, they found it necessary to view him as an unworthy individual, whose punishment was made inevitable by his own deficiencies of character' (p. 27). Sometimes the mechanics of punishment, beginning with an initial reaction of suspicion or hostility, generate their own vindictive momentum.

When we think about the soldiers who inflicted the scourging on Jesus, we now start to see them not as monsters utterly different from us, but human beings just like us, whose real fault is blinding themselves to the humanity of other people. Sometimes such blindness is a defence mechanism – when Comic Relief night comes round again, how long will it be before the sight of other people's hardships becomes unendurable? That's the point at which we either get our credit card out and reach for the phone, or grab the remote control and switch the television off, so as not to have to see the suffering any more. Sometimes we are not really blind at all –

we do see someone else being bullied and mocked but we are too frightened to protest in case we become the next victim.

Why did Jesus have to die? In the garden of Gethsemane, we saw that the 'have' was not generated by a death wish or rebellious streak. With the scourging of Jesus we see that his death was driven from without, by the nature of authority, by human suspicion of what is different, by human resentment of challenges to the status quo; and by the sheer feebleness of the human conscience. Contemplating the scourging of Christ brings home to us, as nothing else can, what it meant for the one who was in the form of God to be incarnate, truly human. His pain embraces and redeems everything we shall ever have to endure. His scourging reminds us that this redemption includes pain inflicted as a matter of banal, routine injustice, because no one could be bothered, and no one cared enough, to do what was just instead of what was easy.

Questions for further thought and discussion

1 Why do you think God allowed Jesus to suffer?
2 Is God unfair?
3 Why is forgiveness so difficult?
4 What do you think you would have done if you had taken part in the Milgram experiment?

A prayer for the mystery of the scourging of Jesus

God our Father,
in the pain inflicted so unjustly on your Son,
I can see the injustice of the world
in which so many live in poverty and hunger,
and in the shadow of war.
Turn my compassion into action,
for the sake of Jesus Christ our Lord. Amen.

3

The crowning with thorns

Mark 15.16–20
Then the soldiers led him into the courtyard of the palace (that is, the governor's headquarters); and they called together the whole cohort. And they clothed him in a purple cloak; and after twisting some thorns into a crown, they put it on him. And they began saluting him, 'Hail, King of the Jews!' They struck his head with a reed, spat upon him, and knelt down in homage to him. After mocking him, they stripped him of the purple cloak and put his own clothes on him. Then they led him out to crucify him.

The second sorrowful mystery, the scourging of Jesus, was about routine injustice and the banality of human cruelty. The third, the crowning of Jesus with thorns, develops this theme, moving on to yet more difficult ground. The Gospels are clear that the crowning with thorns was an act of deliberate corporate spite, designed to humiliate someone who was totally powerless.

It cannot be denied that human beings are capable of great cruelty, especially when they are under stress, or feel threatened. We all know it in theory, but we are reluctant to accept the evidence of such cruelty when it reflects badly on those we are closely associated with. The ease with which we commit evil acts when we feel that our safety or security is at risk is most apparent (though not by any means exclusively so) in warfare.

Every Remembrance Day, Christians and non-Christians alike gather to reflect on the paradox of warfare: that it brings out the best and the worst in us. The best we can easily recall from the words of Jesus himself, 'No one has greater love than this, to lay down one's life for one's friends' (John 15.13). He spoke these words on the eve of his execution. They are prefaced by the reiteration of words first found in John 13.34: 'I give you a new commandment, that you love one another. Just as I have loved you, you also should love one another. By this everyone will know that you are my disciples, if you have love for one another.' (In Latin, this new commandment is called the *mandatum novum*, from which Maundy Thursday gets its name.)

The best that warfare brings out in people is that fear will bind us together because it evokes the awareness and power of love. As I mentioned before, St Paul tells us that love is the greatest of the 'three things which last for ever' (1 Corinthians 13.13). The eternal nature of love draws us to God, because it is the part of our nature which is in the divine image – loving makes us God-like. Love, especially love expressed through sacrifice of the self, is truly divine; it bears the mark of God's very essence. That's the best of human nature in time of war, or when under imminent threat.

What of the worst of human nature? There are all too many examples to choose from – Idi Amin, Pol Pot, Stalin and Hitler are notorious examples from history. We could add plenty of names from recent years to that list. Since the second Iraq war, a trickle of stories has exposed the dark side of military occupation of that land. There have been thousands of civilian and military deaths, enough to populate a sizeable city. And all those dead human individuals had families and loved ones to grieve, or to perish with them, or to live the rest of their lives in sorrow and resentment. The numbers are hard to imagine. When I was speaking about these abuses to people in Norwich

Cathedral, I asked them to consider what those kinds of numbers might mean in terms of their own city and community. It meant one in four people dead. One in four children in each local school, dead. One in four in the streets where people lived, dead. Nothing in our experience since the Blitz has approached this level of mass bereavement, destruction and fear. And the conflict in Iraq is not unique; it is typical.

Other, even darker stories have emerged from Iraq, and these stories fit the theme of the crowning with thorns depressingly well. The most notorious example (though others could be given) is the torture and abuse of Iraqi prisoners by US soldiers in the notorious Abu Ghraib prison in 2004. But the injustices perpetrated there are typical of the cruelty that fear and war can drive human beings to commit. When news of the torture of Iraqi prisoners by US soldiers first broke, I did not look further into it because I was reluctant to deal with the moral discomfort of being a part (however passively) of an alliance responsible for such abuses. But eventually I decided to see for myself, and looked up the images on the internet: an unmuzzled dog used to frighten a prisoner; prisoners' bodies showing marks from dog bites; soldiers kneeling on prisoners; soldiers watching as prisoners try to maintain agonizing postures while stripped naked.*

These photographs speak to us with great immediacy and force and show us human nature at its worst. They are not easy to contemplate, but neither is it easy to explore the depths of the crowning with thorns. Both events share a common theme: the opposition of the powerless and the powerful; the vulnerable at the mercy of the strong. When I looked at the photographs from Abu Ghraib one stood out: a tall, muscular

---

* They can be viewed at <http://commons.wikimedia.org/wiki/Category:Abu_Ghraib_prisoner_abuse_images>.

soldier, carrying a baton, stood before a prisoner who was covered in a 'brown substance'. One figure was big, the other small; one was dominant, the other cowering; one was relaxed; the other had his arms stretched out and one leg crossed over the other, in exactly the posture we associate with the crucified Jesus. Striking as this parallel was, what was most haunting about this image was something else, something *universally* comprehensible. One figure was naked, the other fully clothed.

There is no simpler way to assert your dominance over another person than to strip them of clothing, of everything that sets us apart from animals, everything by which we declare our individuality and personality. Clothing is a form of protection, and an expression of our need to be private. We disclose our selves when we remove it, we become vulnerable, because in our nakedness nothing stands between us and the scorn and mockery of others. This is no matter of mere vanity. It is not that, if our bodies were perfect, we would not care about nakedness. Adam and Eve in the garden of Eden were naked but not ashamed, because they had no knowledge of shame. Like children, their nakedness caused them no concern – until their eyes were opened, and they saw the world as adults see it.

In this fallen world, bodies are a commodity, more or less valuable according to their shape and colour and size. Bodies can be exploited, giving pleasure at a price. In this world, the business of sex is so fraught with danger that an institution like marriage had to evolve to protect individuals from the immeasurable damage and suffering we can inflict through the expression of our desires. In this world, bodies can be objects of scorn, held cheap, as well as objects of obsession as plastic surgery holds out to the desperate the vain hope of physical perfection. Bodies can be sites of pain and suffering, for the sadistic and perverted pleasure of others. And bodies can be a way of bolstering the egos of the cruel and dominant.

What does this show? Surely not that US soldiers are more cruel than the soldiers of other nations, or that soldiers are more cruel than civilians, or that modern society is more cruel than ancient society. All that has changed is the visibility of the cruelty. In all this, the real constant in human affairs is sin. One of the apocryphal books of the Bible declares, 'pride is the root of every sin' (Ecclesiasticus 10.13). This sharp, perceptive statement is true in two ways. Pride is thinking of ourselves more highly than we ought to think, so that first we fail to recognize God in other people and second we fail to recognize that we are not God. Pride is the sin which puts us, our selves, our views, our feelings and ideas, in God's place (which is to say, at the centre of our life). It assumes that what we think, God our Father must also think. So pride is closely tied to the primal sin – idolatry. To worship that which is not God is not a trivial mistake but an immense blasphemy. So is failing to accord worth to that which is made in God's image. In our culture, where faith in God is no longer at the centre of life for most people, all that seems left to put in its place is ourselves.

Every human being on the planet, every human being who has ever lived, is made in the image and likeness of God. Even the poor, the 'ugly', the 'stupid'. Even the vain, the selfish, the proud and the cruel. Certainly the enemy we face in battle; certainly the tormentor who abuses us. This is the clear teaching of the Bible. Being in God's image and likeness is nothing to do with ideas or beliefs. It is simply what we are. If we fail to recognize this truth, we fall into the sin of pride – we begin to regard some people as more precious or valuable than others, and conversely, some lives as cheaper and more expendable than others.

I am not trying to suggest that all people are the same. That is demonstrably untrue. Nor am I saying that all people are equally useful, or contribute equally to the good of society as a whole. But we all participate in the divine likeness. That likeness is the same likeness which Jesus showed most clearly, because, being the incarnate son of God, he embodied with absolute perfection the image of God. His divinity and humanity were in perfect concord, as ours are not. So how did Jesus image God to us?

He emptied himself, taking the form of a slave. He got down on his knees and washed our feet, the servant of all. He who was transfigured on the mountain-top, robed in dazzling white, who walked on water and raised the dead and fed the multitude, accepted imprisonment, judgement, flogging, mockery and nakedness. He was taken into the soldiers' barracks, naked and beaten. His culture held that nakedness was shameful, that to be seen naked by others was wrong. The same would be true of the Iraqi detainees, photographed naked before each other by their captors.

In a travesty of human sympathy, those Roman soldiers gave Jesus something to cover himself with – and no rag either, but a fine robe, a robe of imperial purple. Wrapped in the purple, he was given a crown made of sharp thorns, and (in St Matthew's account) a reed to hold, like a sceptre – and they laughed at him. They mocked and scorned him, and jeered at the title which others had given to him – 'Hail, King of the Jews!' I am sure that when they did so, they looked just like the soldiers in the Abu Ghraib photographs, tough and scary and fully clothed, humiliating the vulnerable and naked.

Sometimes when soldiers are held to account for atrocities such as these, they will say, 'I didn't want to take part, I just didn't know how to stand out against the crowd. All my friends were doing it.' If we look again at the text of Mark, we find a telling detail. The soldiers who were on duty had scourged Jesus, probably as a routine punishment, and in all likelihood without the deliberate spite and sadism which Mel Gibson depicted in his film. But after this, the soldiers led Jesus away inside the palace, and 'they called together the whole cohort'. When it comes to inflicting cruelty, it helps to be part of a crowd.

So the crowning of Jesus with a plaited wreath of thorns still has power to shock us today because it speaks to our half-hidden sense of our ingrained human sinfulness, to our temptation to submerge our own individual responsibility for wrongdoing in what we do corporately, instead of being ready to justify our actions, and defend our behaviour, as individuals.

By now, we are beginning to see that the Passion story has a timeless universality about it. It is a story which affected people long ago at the core of their being; and it has exactly the same effect on us. Many men and women have found in the Passion story the courage to speak out against wrongdoing, and the courage to suffer and endure evil. One of the great reformers of the Church of England, Thomas Cranmer, is just such a person. He died in 1556, burned alive because of what he believed and wrote about God and the Church. Cranmer is a particularly interesting example, because of his failures. He was a shrewd political operator – he kept his head, literally as well as metaphorically, which was no mean feat considering he served Henry VIII for twenty years. Eventually he gave in to pressure to say what he did not believe, but after doing so, he later recanted. It takes great courage not to commit sin; it also takes courage to step away from a sin committed and to decide not to sin again.

Cranmer was caught up in great matters of state, and the pressing issues of his day. But today, fighting over, and dying for, the principles for which he was condemned seems dis-proportionate or even meaningless. Perhaps one day the big issues of our time will seem likewise. But the Passion does not only speak to great matters of state, global issues, or general truths of human nature. It speaks to our individual experience, and to our everyday lives. And the third sorrowful mystery, the crowning with thorns, urges us to think about the inner dispositions of the human heart, and its propensity for wrong-doing. When we hear the story of the soldiers mocking Jesus, what do we think of? At present I think first of those Abu Ghraib pictures, of soldiers mocking and humiliating prisoners. But before I had seen them, other images and ideas were in my mind, for example, stories and films in which groups (which everyone aspires to join, or fears exclusion from) isolate or torment the vulnerable outsider – *Lord of the Flies*, *Carrie*, *Master and Commander* – or graphic illustrations of bestial cruelty in paintings by Altdorfer, Bosch, Tissot and Titian. Titian shows Jesus crowned with thorns and seated beneath a bust of Tiberius Caesar crowned with laurel, to contrast the earthly kingship of the then Roman emperor with the suffering and sorrows of Jesus the King of the Jews. Such visual impressions imprint on our minds the terror of unprovoked hostility. I said earlier that in praying the sorrowful mysteries we must enter imaginatively into the scene being described, and become part of it. If we do this, who do we become? Are we like Jesus – the one mocked and humiliated, laughed to scorn? Or do we find ourselves closer to those soldiers, the ones doing the laughing, the hurting, the humiliating?

We have a special word for the tendency of human beings to terrify and hurt one another. It is applicable to any situation where perpetrator and victim are stuck with one another, where getting away is not an option. We call it 'bullying'. I suspect that no one is entirely unmarked by the experience of bullying. The very word 'bullying' conjures up stark images of children, some picked on, others doing the taunting and terrifying. I recall talking to a former teacher who was training for the ministry with me. We were discussing the problem of someone in college who somehow didn't 'fit in'. People made an effort, and so I should hope, seeing that they were going to be ministers of God; but they were never at ease with this person, never completely comfortable. This former teacher said to me, 'There are always some children like that in any class. You can't make them fit in; all you can do is make sure the other children don't bully them.'

'Fitting in' is a fundamental desire for almost all of us. If we think again of the Milgram experiment, we recall how deeply ingrained is our wish to comply with those we see as having authority over us. It is often said that children can be very cruel. This is true. But what really separates adults from children is that children have not yet learned to hide their bullying as adults do. Many of us will recognize in our childhood selves a victim of bullying. Some of us will know, more shamefully, that we were bullies ourselves. Yet bullying is not something we grow out of when we leave the playground. It is endemic in our world, inherent in our fallen human nature. The word we associate with childhood, and children's behaviour, can apply just as appropriately to adults. We must not let the word itself deceive us into thinking this is a phenomenon of childhood. It is common in everyday working life. A professor of occupational psychology has said that there are two types of workplace bully: the type who need to put people down in order to boost their own self-esteem; and the type who feel overloaded and stressed and may not realize that their actions are perceived as bullying. Both categories reveal that bullies are victims as well as perpetrators.

The Bible speaks of the sins of the fathers being visited on the children; and the Church used to talk about original sin being transmitted from one generation to the next. I think this is a way of saying that we *become* what we *experience*. This suggests that being treated cruelly teaches us to be cruel; that dehumanizing treatment reduces our ability to empathize –

that is, to imagine what it is like to be someone else, and to behave to someone else as though their pain, like our own, is real. On the other hand, when our human relationships are fruitful and creative, they teach us to evoke and communicate love, through the vital media of forgiveness, patience, tolerance. This too can be handed down by parents to their children, from one generation to another.

The soldiers plaited a crown of thorns and placed it on Jesus' head. They were laughing at his self-identity; jeering at who he believed himself to be; trying to undermine his very sense of who he was. They were made less human by acting less humanely. They found the mocking and jeering easier to carry out because they were not acting alone but as a group – diluting the guilt. Yet every cruel action has an effect. The effect may seem to be transient: those of us who are bullies can grow out of it; those of us who are bullied move on, get over it. But the scars are lifelong. The effects on our personalities, our inmost fears, our outward mechanisms for coping with the pressures of daily life – these are never entirely healed, even when the suffering has passed out of mind. Just as every act of cruelty we endure has a cumulative effect on our soul's health, so sin itself is cumulative: committing sin gets easier every time we give in, and harder to resist.

In what does the sin of Abu Ghraib, or the sin of that cohort of Roman soldiers, or the sin of everyday bullying consist? In each case, the evil is the same: to put ourselves in the place of God. To refuse to see the image of God in other people. To turn a blind eye to abuses inflicted on others. To exercise our God-given strength and power to make others suffer, instead of showing them compassion. All this is sin. It points us towards the ever-present reality of sin – that is, our human tendency to be corrupted by the temptation to conform, to disguise our vulnerability by finding someone, anyone weaker than ourselves, and making them pay the price for our fears. All this is sin. So sin is a denial of the divine image in us and in other people. And the price paid for that is the highest price imaginable – the death of God incarnate.

When Jesus was crowned with thorns, he endured what most of us fear more than physical pain. Humiliation, shame and ridicule are so painful that things which happened to us in earliest childhood are unforgettably incised on our memories, like ugly scars which never really heal. Instead they haunt us, so that sometimes adult life is a flight from those memories, a cloaking of our real, vulnerable selves, based on a determination never again to experience such vulnerability. All the more extraordinary, therefore, is the fact that Jesus accepted such shame willingly, for our sakes: 'Though he was in the form of God, he did not regard equality with God as something to be exploited, but emptied himself, taking the form of a slave, being born in human likeness' (Philippians 2.6).

Questions for further thought and discussion

1 What should Pontius Pilate have done about Jesus?
2 Is bullying an inevitable part of human society?
3 Can we learn from history, or only repeat it?
4 How can we learn to see the image of God in every human being?

A prayer for the mystery of the crowning with thorns

God our Father,
it is a terrible thing to endure mockery and shame.
May I never be ashamed of the Gospel,
or of the name of 'Christian';
grant me courage to stand out against the majority for the
   sake of right,
through Jesus Christ our Lord. Amen.

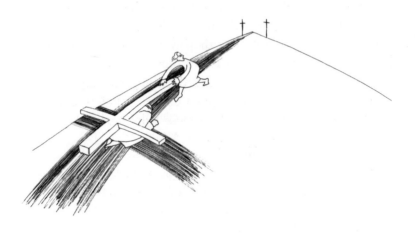

4

The carrying of the cross

———•◦•———

Mark 15.21–25
They compelled a passer-by, who was coming in from the country, to carry his cross; it was Simon of Cyrene, the father of Alexander and Rufus. Then they brought Jesus to the place called Golgotha (which means the place of a skull). And they offered him wine mixed with myrrh; but he did not take it. And they crucified him, and divided his clothes among them, casting lots to decide what each should take.

It was nine o'clock in the morning when they crucified him.

As we journey deeper into the sorrowful mysteries, we are like people reading a novel, aware that they have left the halfway point behind, as the handful of pages on the right hand side gets thinner than that on the left; or like people praying the rosary, who can feel from their beads that three mysteries are past, and only two are left to pray. If you are reading one chapter of this book each week for Lenten study, then by now Lent is more than half gone, and Holy Week is drawing closer. In our own way, we Lenten pilgrims are like Jesus on the way of sorrows – we walk towards horror and suffering with our eyes open, in full knowledge of what awaits him, and us, on Calvary hill. We prepare ourselves spiritually and intellectually, as best we may, for the rigours of Holy Week, and above all, for the prayers of Good Friday. With the fourth sorrowful mystery, the carrying of the cross, we have found the right moment to ask how we understand the 'Christ-event', and how we explain it to ourselves and to others.

When we become Christians, we do so in one of two basic ways. We are brought up as Christians, or we are later converted to Christianity. Either way, we have to assimilate one fundamental principle: that God has acted in our life to call us to himself. From this we also have to take on the idea that God does this despite our character faults and sinful habits, things which all Christians ought to be sharply aware of. One of the fundamental beliefs of all Christians is that we cannot earn salvation by good works – in other words we cannot buy God's favour by what we do. We are saved by his undeserved favour – for which the technical term is 'grace'. That grace is 'prevenient' – which is to say, it goes before us. It is not reactive (to our behaviour) but aboriginal (part of the way God has created the world and us). It reaches out to us before we make what we think is the first move to God. As far as theories of salvation go, many people get this far, and feel no need to go further. There is nothing wrong with this. Many people have an inner conviction of being saved, a close dependence on Jesus Christ as the one through whom this 'being saved', this 'salvation', has happened. And for them, this is enough. They do not feel any need to analyse these beliefs in order to understand them more deeply.

Why is it all right to stop there? Because faith is a gift freely given, to be joyfully accepted. It does not have to be bolstered or 'improved' by intellectual enquiry. There are other ways of deepening faith, not all of them academic or even verbal, such as prayer and service, to name but two. This is not to say that no one should bother to explore the meaning of their faith in more depth. The 'all may, none must, some should' principle

is fitting here. For some, faith which is not explored will stag-
nate; for others, there is no sense of a need to question what
God has given them, to take it apart to see how it works, or
to try to strengthen it. There is a risk that applying the intellect
may destroy the genuine experience – like a favourite poem
subjected to literary-critical analysis. This dilemma makes
me think of Walt Whitman's poem, 'When I Heard the Learn'd
Astronomer':

> When I heard the learn'd astronomer;
> When the proofs, the figures, were ranged in columns before
>   me;
> When I was shown the charts and the diagrams, to add, divide,
>   and measure them;
> When I, sitting, heard the astronomer, where he lectured with
>   much applause in the lecture-room,
> How soon, unaccountable, I became tired and sick;
> Till rising and gliding out, I wander'd off by myself,
> In the mystical moist night-air, and from time to time,
> Looked up in perfect silence at the stars.

Understanding is gained, but at the price of the sense of mystery, distance, and transcendence, which is what made the
thing wonderful in the first place. It is not surprising if people
worry that applying intellectual theories to faith-experiences will
spoil or diminish them.

On the other hand, we need to believe that our faith is
reasonable, and may be expressed in terms which are neither
incoherent nor anti-intellectual. Unfortunately, the gap between
academic theology and devotional writing can be wide. And
the number of Christian writers who manage to bridge the
divide is pitifully few. It takes real courage to wrestle with faith
and belief, and real trust to let go of the old certainties and
reach out to God without knowing where the next step will
take us. In the end, the only thing we can be sure of is that the

reality of God is something utterly beyond the power of human expression.

Some Christians believe that we do not need theories to explain salvation in Jesus Christ because everything that we need to know is in the Bible. And in a sense that is true. Everything we need *is* in the Bible – but we still need tools to make sense of all the evidence, all the material we have to hand. It is like taking flat-pack furniture home and finding that the instructions are all in diagram form – they are supposed to be understood by anyone in any language, but in fact you have to know the pictorial *conventions* in order to make sense of the *instructions*. Still, this is a sensitive subject. If one needs to understand the theories which underpin Christian faith, does that mean that only theologians and Bible scholars can be saved? What about ordinary people who don't have shelves full of commentaries and theological tomes?

I cannot say that theology and biblical studies have made no difference to my faith. They have made a difference and furthered my understanding. For instance, even a basic knowledge of Hebrew opens up the Old Testament in a very exciting way; and reading the New Testament in Greek can be a profound, humbling experience. Much more importantly, reading the original languages of the scriptures also gives Christian preachers and teachers tools for making sense of the Bible for other people. I am grateful that being able to read the Bible in this way has deepened and informed my faith. But there was a time when I had not learned Greek and Hebrew. Was I a less sincere Christian then? Did I say my prayers less devoutly? Did I know Jesus Christ as my personal saviour less clearly? Of course not. The Bible itself teaches us that faith is not simply a matter of knowledge. Knowledge of scripture is like good behaviour. It is a lovely by-product of a life of discipleship. But knowledge is not a substitute for discipleship.

So do we need theories to help us understand our own salvation? The short answer is, no. We do not *need* to understand or explain our salvation for it to be real. If we want to communicate our faith, however – to explain it to others, to defend it against attacks from outside and doubts within – we had better be well prepared. And that means finding words in which to explain what God brought about through the death of Jesus, what difference the Passion has made to human history, and to us as individuals – in other words, a theory.

Let me begin by saying that no single theory perfectly fits the facts, or fully explains the events of the Passion for all generations past, present and future. As time goes on, and the world changes, different theories seem to fit the facts of our salvation more or less closely. This is because we can only understand God in terms of our own experience – and our language for speaking about God cannot keep pace with our way of understanding God. Christian language is protected and hallowed by centuries of liturgical practice and prayer; so it is slow to change. We prefer the old words: just ask any congregation which has to cope with a new prayer book or hymn-book. But our ideas and concepts *do* change, and the fact that the *words* don't can mask and disguise the fact.

Of course, some of our terminology for God is unchanging over time. The fact that we call God 'Father' is a good example: fatherhood is something universally understood, either by experience or observation. Yet even here the boundaries are changing – 'father' does not always imply the unquestioned head or the clear authority figure it once did. But however imperfect our earthly fathers may be, we all find it possible to hold in our minds an image of the perfect heavenly Father, though nowadays our ideal Father is likely to be characterized more by love than by authority. Other terms for God are less universal – King, Lord and Judge, for

51

example. These make perfect sense in a pre-modern society with a strong hierarchy and clear social divisions. They are now much less immediate in the way they image God to us, for our society is – at least in theory – more egalitarian. Of course we still use the language of kingship and lordship, but we do so figuratively, as people in a society which has nothing to fear from the exercise of a monarch's dominion or a lord's power. So too with Shepherd. We use the language of the shepherd, but our understanding of God shepherding his people, so clear to the people of the Old Testament, cannot be grounded in everyday experience – at least, not for most of us. Many Christians who think of Jesus with trust and affection as the Good Shepherd have never even seen a real shepherd.

Thus the language of 'redemption' and 'ransom', so long familiar, has sometimes been regarded by Christians as literal, and at other times, including nowadays, as obviously meta-phorical. Just as we know what we mean when we call Jesus a good shepherd, or depict him as one (and it is not that we imagine him tending actual sheep), so in the case of 'ransom' and 'redemption', calling them metaphors is *not* the same thing as saying that they are not really true. It will be important to bear this in mind when we come to the sacrifice of Christ on the cross.

Religious language changes very, very slowly; but human conceptions of God are changing all the time, according to our circumstances and experience. And it has always been that way. We can see exactly this process working itself out within the Old Testament, and even, to a lesser extent, in the New Testament. No labels are adequate for God. Perhaps it was because of this that Jesus 'emptied himself, taking the form of a slave'. While all else is changing in societies and cultures over time, one thing – it seems – is a constant throughout history. As Jesus himself reminds us in the Gospels, we will always have the poor with us. There will always be someone somewhere who is hungry, beaten, mocked, outcast, treated unjustly. So the image of the crucified Christ never ceases to speak directly to us, just like the image of God the Father.

Theories of what happened on the cross, what God wrought by it, are called 'atonement' theories. Over the centuries the Church has reflected on the meaning of the Passion, and the outcome of all that thought and reflection has been the teaching we now know by that name. For once, the popular etymology is not wrong: atonement really does mean 'making at-one', healing and uniting what has been fractured and divided. 'Atonement' is the only central term of theology which is English in origin. Theories of the atonement attempt to explain:

- why Jesus died;
- why God allowed it to happen;
- what was achieved by Jesus' death.

Yet when we start to explore atonement, we cannot start with the Passion. The first Christians – we can never say this too often – saw everything to do with Jesus *in the light of the resurrection*. Their faith, their understanding, their desire to reach out to others, were all conditioned by the absolute, overwhelming conviction that 'God has made him both Lord and Messiah, this Jesus whom you crucified' (Acts 2.36). They began from the resurrection. They built on their experiences of the risen Lord. They saw the world as having been changed for ever by the fact of the resurrection, as death was undone. Without the benefit of hundreds of years of careful argument, they saw a simple, clear connection between the fact of the resurrection and Jesus' acceptance of death as – somehow – necessary and right. From this connection, they drew two conclusions: first, that Jesus was divine, and second (our topic here) that his death had loosed the hold of death on all humanity.

So they began from a conviction of faith, and as good Jews they looked to the sacred writings of their people for clues to the meaning of what they had experienced. They found several scriptures relevant to our theme, two in particular.

One gives a picture of the willing acceptance of suffering and humiliation:

> I gave my back to those who struck me,
>> and my cheeks to those who pulled out the beard;
> I did not hide my face
>> from insult and spitting. (Isaiah 50.6)

This evokes our first three sorrowful mysteries – the agony in the garden; the scourging; and the crowning with thorns.

The second passage has more to say:

> He was despised and rejected by others;
>> a man of suffering and acquainted with infirmity;
> and as one from whom others hide their faces
>> he was despised, and we held him of no account.
> Surely he has borne our infirmities
>> and carried our diseases;
> yet we accounted him stricken,
>> struck down by God, and afflicted.
> But he was wounded for our transgressions,
>> crushed for our iniquities;
> upon him was the punishment that made us whole,
>> and by his bruises we are healed.
> All we like sheep have gone astray;
>> we have all turned to our own way,
> and the Lord has laid on him
>> the iniquity of us all. (Isaiah 53.3–6)

This text yields an extraordinary answer: the Lord has laid on him the iniquity of us all. This is a theory of *exchange*: with his wounds we are healed. Applying this famous text to our faith can put Christians in severe difficulty. We may start where the first followers started, and where, I suggested, we all must start: with a conviction that God has called us into relationship through Jesus. With the conviction voiced by Peter, that, 'this Jesus, once crucified, is Lord and Messiah'. But we also believe that the God who calls us is good, and just, and that he loves us all. How can this good, loving God allow the punishment of the righteous? How can he permit the innocent to suffer? In particular, how can he permit the undeserved suffering of his Son? If we are to maintain belief in the goodness and justice of God, something has to give. That something is us.

The Jewish people, when in exile in Babylon, asked 'Why?' They could not accept the answer that God was at fault, that his love or justice had failed; and so they located the fault in themselves, their apostasy, their rejection of the covenant. So it is also with Christians. We begin from the fact of the crucifixion. And we too ask 'Why?' No more than our Jewish forebears can we accept that God is to blame, that his love and his justice have failed. So we locate the fault in the only other place we think we can – in ourselves. Drawing upon these texts from Isaiah, we feel forced to conclude that it is because of us – our sinfulness, our wickedness – that Jesus died, and that this is what Isaiah means when he writes that the suffering one was 'wounded for our transgressions'; and that 'the LORD has laid on him the iniquity of us all'.

So the passage from Isaiah not only prefigures the suffering of Jesus, it appears to offer an explanation for it. There is a direct causal relationship between what *we* (humankind) have done, and what *he* suffered; *and* God has done this to him, *and* by what God has done to him, and what he accepted, we are healed (or, putting it another way, we are saved). To make sense of this, think back to the second and third sorrowful mysteries: Jesus' physical torment in being beaten and stripped, and his emotional torment in being mocked. In this light these appear to be things he accepted, to save us from having to suffer such punishment.

At this point, I have to say, we really need to pause. The implications of this line of thought are unimaginably serious and terrible. All that anguish, all that suffering and torment, all that humiliation. Did God really make that happen to his own Son Jesus? Harder still, did he do it because, if Jesus had not taken our place, God would have made us suffer so instead? According to the view of many Christians, the answer to those questions is 'yes'. God did allow his own Son to be tortured to death: he did so because he was angry with us for our sinfulness, and his justice demanded that someone should be punished. Jesus bore the punishment which should have been ours, to satisfy God's righteous anger.

This view of the atonement is called the 'penal substitution' theory: 'penal' because Jesus paid a penalty, suffered a punishment; 'substitution' because he substituted himself for us, who should have paid that penalty, and suffered that punishment. This theory of the atonement was first set down by certain Reformation theologians, especially John Calvin, in the sixteenth century. It became the established view of many Protestant churches. This view is based on a belief that God is angry with humankind for its wickedness. There is considerable scriptural evidence in the Old Testament for this perception of God as angry, and also some in the New Testament – Romans 5.9, for example. The penal substitution theory tries to explain how the death of Jesus put human-kind and God 'at one' again. According to this theory, Jesus achieved this by substituting himself in our place, accepting a punishment we should have suffered, though he, of course, was wholly innocent. One Anglican theologian dismisses the theory as a 'legal fiction', by which Jesus' 'righteousness is "imputed" to us and our guilt is "imputed" to him', so that 'he suffers vicariously for us'. He concludes – and I agree – that 'such a harsh, even tyrannical, picture of God is unacceptable', and 'sub-Christian' (Macquarrie, 1990, p. 401).

To try to offer a full exploration of alternative ideas would carry us far beyond the scope of this book. All that needs to be said here is that virtually everyone would agree that justice is not justice if it punishes the innocent in place of the guilty, even when the innocent are willing to accept such punishment (as for example a parent might, to save their child). There are other, better ways of understanding human sinfulness, as endemic, universal: as seeing the willing self-offering of Jesus not as appeasing the wrath of an angry God in order to protect us, but rather as stepping into the mire of human wickedness to carry us across it – not only taking upon him our burdens, but carrying us to safety. Perhaps Paul gave us a glimpse into how we might learn to imitate Jesus in this respect when he wrote, 'Bear one another's burdens, and in this way you will fulfil the law of Christ' (Galatians 6.2).

The fourth sorrowful mystery points us directly to this alternative understanding of the atonement. Usually, this mystery is prayed by focusing on Christ carrying his cross. The image is of the cross as a burden to Jesus himself, a means of salvation for us. His tree of shame becomes our tree of victory. But I would like to focus on the relationship between Christ and Simon of Cyrene. Remember that Jesus began his walk from the place of his torment in the praetorium, where he was beaten and mocked. Now, as was customary, he carried the instrument of his execution. He had not eaten; he had not slept; he must have been weak from pain, fatigue, loss of blood. Perhaps the soldiers became worried that he would not make it to Golgotha at all, that he would die on the way. Perhaps he was just too slow, and they wanted to get on with the business, so they could knock off for the day, and go home and put their feet up. Whatever the reason, we know, from the accounts of Matthew, Mark and Luke, that the soldiers grabbed Simon of Cyrene from the crowd and made him carry the cross for Jesus.

Mark tells us this Simon was 'the father of Alexander and Rufus', as if his readers knew who Alexander and Rufus were. Perhaps they were part of the group of first Christians in Rome. It is possible that the very act of carrying the cross for Jesus brought Simon into discipleship, and his sons with him. It is in this part of the story that we can find a further clue to the meaning of the Passion for us today. Jesus carried his cross, and when he could not, Simon carried it for him. But he did not *offer* to carry the cross for Jesus: the soldiers made him do so. Simon may have been picked at random by the soldiers. It may be that he was singled out because, as tradition has it, he was black (Cyrene is in Africa). In this tiny fragment of detail from the Gospel story, we begin to glimpse humanity co-operating with the work of Christ, sharing in the essence of Christ's work by accepting the burden another was bound to carry.

I have already said that it is a fundamental truth of Christian faith that we cannot earn our salvation by what we do. Our relationship with God is a covenant, not a contract. But while we cannot earn our salvation by acts of kindness, or generosity, or self-denial, a Christian ought to show all these virtues, just the same. The grace of God is prevenient. His undeserved favour towards human beings comes before any action or reaction on our part. We cannot earn our salvation, because it was wrought in Christ in the beginning, when the Word already was. Still, it was actualized at the right moment in history. So although we cannot earn our salvation, and although we cannot deserve it, we can still co-operate in our salvation, by conforming ourselves to the likeness of Christ, who took 'the form of a slave, being born in human likeness' (Philippians 2.7).

If the ancient traditions of the Church are to be trusted – and I think they are – Simon was not the only person who helped Jesus on his way. There is another story in the Passion not recorded in the Gospels, but extremely ancient (it dates from the fourth century) – that a woman called Veronica, perhaps the woman with an issue of blood whom Jesus healed, came forward from the crowd and wiped Jesus' face. This story witnesses to the same faith among the early Christians that individual people could and would co-operate with Jesus in the burden he had accepted, and would contribute what lay within their power to forwarding the work of Christ.

This is in no sense a matter of earning salvation. It is more a matter of what the pre-Christian philosopher Aristotle called 'recognition' (*anagnorisis*). Aristotle used this word when analysing tragic drama, to refer to the moment when one character recognizes the true identity of another – and also, to a character's realization of another character's true significance. One character in the Passion story who experiences a clear moment of recognition is the penitent thief on the cross beside Jesus – tradition has it that his name was Dismas. He recognized in Jesus the truth, that here was the king of Israel: 'Jesus, remember me when you come into your kingdom' (Luke 23.42). Never mind that Dismas was crucified as a justly convicted criminal. His recognition of Jesus as the true King has its reward, and Jesus' words of mercy to Dismas echo down the centuries: 'Truly I tell you, today you will be with me in Paradise' (Luke 23.42–43). Nor is Dismas alone. There is also the moment of recognition in which an unnamed woman pours perfume on

Jesus, and he says 'her sins, which are many, are forgiven; for she loved much' (Luke 7.4, Revised Standard Version). There is the calling of Matthew the tax-collector (Matthew 9.9); Peter at Caesarea Philippi (Mark 8.27); and the centurion at the foot of the cross (Mark 15.39). And after the resurrection there are others: Thomas, whose moment of recognition comes when he confesses Jesus as 'My Lord and my God' (John 20.28); Mary Magdalene and her recognition in the garden – 'Rabbouni!' (John 20.16); Cleopas and his companion on the road to Emmaus (Luke 24.31); and Paul himself, on the road to Damascus (Acts 9.3–6). Christ discloses in himself the very nature of God. He discloses it to all. But not all respond with recognition: those who have ears to hear, let them hear!

For Jesus this kind of recognition of God is a fundamental feature of true repentance, as we see in his parable of the Pharisee and the tax-collector (Luke 18.9–14). The recognition of the true nature of the divine brings with it an overwhelming clarity of vision – as we see ourselves for the first time for what we really are, stripped of all pretence, the mask of lies and self-importance with which we try to shield ourselves from the pain of adult living. Remember the words with which the tax-collector in the parable recognizes God: 'God, be merciful to me, a sinner' (Luke 18.13).

In any life of faith, two things must go together – a recognition of the holiness and goodness of God, and a recognition of how far we fall short of that holiness and goodness. The crucifixion sets God's holiness against our unrighteousness. We have already considered the reality of evil, through the second and third sorrowful mysteries – evil perpetrated, and perpetuated, through human reluctance to stand out from the crowd. Human fear of punishment or criticism. Human readiness to obey orders, even to the point of cruelty. Human malice and readiness to taunt and despise the vulnerable, instead of having compassion. All this manifold sin and wickedness is before us. But there is another reality, the meaning and scope of which are shown in the carrying of the cross and the imminent crucifixion: absolute love, absolute goodness, absolute compassion; absolute trust in God. And all this despite the agony of knowing that it could all have been different; despite the scourging and mockery; despite the burden of the cross – on one level a piece of wood, on another the symbol of the suffering of the world, shouldered willingly for the sake of the world's salvation.

We cannot earn our salvation by good works; but we can co-operate in our salvation, by accepting and responding to moments of 'recognition', learning to see the Lord of glory for what he really is. We can work with God, and not against him; we can accept our own need for God instead of standing against him and refusing to respond to his call. We can do so by letting ourselves – like Dismas and Veronica and Simon of Cyrene, and the woman with her perfume – look beyond appearances, beyond an ordinary person, beyond a beaten criminal – and instead to *recognize*, to see as God sees. Only then can we accept the implications of Christ's suffering for us, with our iniquities laid on him; only then can we properly respond to what he actually asks of us – the sincere response which true recognition rightly demands.

Through the fourth sorrowful mystery, we have touched cautiously upon the doctrine of the atonement. I can see why the redeeming work of Christ has been seen as God punishing the just for the unjust; but I do not believe it, because the angry, vengeful God this theory imagines is not a God I recognize. Yet there is great power in such a view of the atonement, precisely because it evokes a sense of guilt, shame, despair, from which faith in Jesus is the only refuge. The penal substitution theory of atonement has been very influential.

But for me this influence comes at too high a price – for it perverts the gospel of love and forgiveness into a message of condemnation.

It is now time to face the heart of our faith – the crucifixion itself – and to finish by interpreting the atonement in terms which make better sense of the justice of God, the sinfulness of humankind, and the love of Jesus.

Questions for further thought and discussion

1 Why bother with theories about salvation and redemption?
2 Can we find new ways of talking about God, and to God? Or are the old ways and old words the best?
3 Is rejecting the penal substitution view of the atonement really just a denial of the plain sense of scripture? Compare Isaiah 53.3–5 with Hosea 11.8–9; Ezekiel 33.11; 1 Peter 3.9.
4 Have you experienced a moment of 'recognition' in your journey to God?

A prayer for the mystery of the carrying of the cross

God our Father,
your Son bore my sins in his own body on the cross.
Give me strength to follow his example,
by helping other people to bear their burdens,
so that I may grow into his likeness,
through the same Jesus Christ our Lord. Amen.

5

The crucifixion

————•◆•————

Mark 15.25–39

It was nine o'clock in the morning when they crucified him. The inscription of the charge against him read, 'The King of the Jews.' And with him they crucified two bandits, one on his right and one on his left. Those who passed by derided him, shaking their heads and saying, 'Aha! You who would destroy the temple and build it in three days, save yourself, and come down from the cross!' In the same way the chief priests, along with the scribes, were also mocking him among themselves and saying, 'He saved others; he cannot save himself. Let the Messiah, the King of Israel, come down from the cross now, so that we may see and believe.' Those who were crucified with him also taunted him.

When it was noon, darkness came over the whole land until three in the afternoon. At three o'clock Jesus cried out with a loud voice, 'Eloi, Eloi, lema sabachthani?' which means, 'My God, my God, why have you forsaken me?' When some of the bystanders heard it, they said, 'Listen, he is calling for Elijah.' And someone ran, filled a sponge with sour wine, put it on a stick, and gave it to him to drink, saying, 'Wait, let us see whether Elijah will come to take him down.' Then Jesus gave a loud cry and breathed his last. And the curtain of the temple was torn in two, from top to bottom. Now when the centurion, who stood facing him, saw that in this way he breathed his last, he said, 'Truly this man was God's Son!'

When we meditate on the crucifixion of Jesus, there is no action taking place in the way there is with the other sorrowful mysteries. The scene before our mind's eye is still. There must have been plenty going on *around* Jesus, of course. Those who loved him stood by watching and weeping. The guards diced and argued. There were people mocking him ('He saved others; he cannot save himself. Let the Messiah, the King of Israel, come down from the cross now, so that we may see and believe', Mark 15.31–32). Others made futile gestures of help ('Someone ran, filled a sponge with sour wine, put it on a stick, and gave it to him to drink', Mark 15.36). But Jesus, nailed there as he was, did nothing active. Instead he spoke. He spoke in agony:

My God, my God, why have you forsaken me? (Mark 15.34);

I thirst (John 19.28).

He spoke in compassion:

Woman, behold your son ... Behold your mother (John 19.26–27);

Today you will be with me in Paradise (Luke 23.43);

Father, forgive them; for they do not know what they are doing (Luke 23.34).

And in moments of sublime mystery, he spoke in prayer:

Father, into your hands I commend my spirit (Luke 23.46);

It is finished (John 19.30).

The meaning of the crucifixion is more in the stillness and solitude than in the words or actions of the scene. Here at last, Jesus goes where even in our imagination we cannot journey with him. The agony of indecision; the dread of punishment; the imprint of cruelty; the weight of burdens to be carried: all this we can to some extent understand, and can sympathize with. But the crucifixion draws us out of the realm of understanding and into that of the divine mystery of love. We can gaze and gaze; but we cannot follow.

All my adult life I have trusted in the power of the cross, and believed in the saving blood of Christ. But what does it *mean*? Atonement theories (the quest for the meaning of the crucifixion) go to the heart of the relationship between God and his creation. They tackle the ultimate questions: What went wrong between God and humankind? What did Jesus do to set that right again?

To recap: everything the first Christians believed about Jesus was grounded in the fact of the resurrection, which they themselves had witnessed. When they began to work through its implications, their ideas of what the resurrection revealed about God, and Jesus, and themselves developed in two directions. On the one hand, they grew into belief in the incarnation – God entering into human flesh, to make humanity divine. On the other they were led to an understanding of the cross as the means of reconciliation and salvation – in other words 'atonement'. So whatever they thought the crucifixion might mean, however they tried to understand it, those first Christians came to see that it had to relate to the incarnation. This is certainly Paul's view, most clearly expressed in 2 Corinthians 5.19: 'God was in Christ [incarnation] reconciling the world to himself [atonement]'. So on one level, the atonement is something which happens *within God*.

Part of the problem with the penal substitution theory of atonement (discussed in the previous chapter) is that it evokes a model of relationship between Father and Son that is hierarchical – the dominant, powerful Father punishes the submissive, powerless Son. On the other hand, it does have the advantage of widening the gap between the roles of Father and Son in the drama of our salvation. If we blur this distinction between Father and Son, and make the atonement something which *only* happens *within* God, then we are in danger of denying the true individuality of Father and Son, and so making God vulnerable to the taint of 'patripassianism' – the idea that God the Father suffered in the crucifixion (something which the early Church worked hard to avoid as it began to formulate the doctrines of Christian faith). Also, if we identify Father and Son too closely, we can fall into the heresy of 'docetism' – denying the reality of Jesus' humanity, regarding it as mere appearance.

At this point, you may be thinking that we are losing touch with reality. What is the point of speculating on these mysteries? Does it matter how we define who did what on the cross? Or how? Perhaps it doesn't seem very important, but believe me, it is. If Christ on the cross was not truly human, fully human, his death has no power to save us, because he is not, in any real sense, *like us*. On the other hand, if Christ on the cross was not truly, fully divine, then his death has no power to save us because he cannot reconnect us with God, cannot bridge the gap between humanity and God. One of the difficulties with the penal substitution view is that it leans too far towards the divinity of Christ, and away from his humanity. This is because penal substitution needs to emphasize the suffering one as being really God, so that there is no injustice in his taking punishment upon himself; he is both the punisher and the punished, and so inflicts and accepts the punishment freely, by his own sovereign choice. It is when we insist that Jesus was truly and fully human too that the idea of his suffering the punishment due to others becomes an injustice in itself, and an affront to the justice of God. The real problem with the substitution theory, as most people intuitively perceive, is that to inflict punishment on one person – even one who accepts it willingly – for sins committed by others is not, and cannot ever be, justice – it cannot resolve the problem of other people's objective moral guilt. A parent might offer, even wish, to suffer in a child's place, to save that child from punishment, out of motives of self-giving love. But we could never regard punishing the parent for the wrongdoing of a child as justice.

Perhaps this is the right moment to press the importance of how the first Christians came to formulate our core beliefs. The main Christian teachings (or 'doctrines') are not complex and paradoxical to make life difficult, or to make ordinary people feel ignorant, or because the theologians who first developed them were more interested in nitpicking intellectualism than Christian discipleship. They are complex and paradoxical because they begin from the complex, paradoxical facts of religious experience, as recorded in scripture and witnessed by generations of the faithful, and they try to formulate in words what Christians believe, based fully and honestly on those experiences.

The God in whom Christians believe is a God of three Persons in one Substance. This formulation of our faith – 'in the name of the Father and of the Son and of the Holy Spirit' – is not an optional extra but a fundamental principle. God the Father and God the Son are separate yet indissoluble. We cannot take easy refuge in the idea that the death of Jesus was merely the setting of a good example by a very, very good man. We are committed to the belief that, in Jesus, the divine entered into human existence, so that somehow (this is where our atonement theories become quite literally *crucial*) when Jesus the God-man is lifted up, he changes for ever the relationship between the divine and human levels of existence. As he himself declares, 'Now is the judgement of this world; now the ruler of this world will be driven out. And I, when I am lifted up from the earth, will draw all people to myself' (John 12.31–32).

In the early days of Christianity, it was pretty much universally believed that God's purity, unity and immutability had to be protected and insisted upon. The reconciling of the world to God could only happen through Jesus Christ, because only he was both true God and true man. So, if we want to get a different angle on the saving work of Christ on the cross from that offered by the penal substitutionary theory of the atonement, the place to begin is the incarnation: 'God was in Christ, reconciling the world to himself'. That verse gives us the incarnation from the viewpoint of God the Father. Another passage of scripture, also written by Paul, shows the incarnation from the point of view of God the Son: 'Let the same mind be in you that was in Christ Jesus, who, though he was in the form of God, did not regard equality with God as something to be exploited, but emptied himself, taking the form of a slave, being born in human likeness' (Philippians 2.6–7).

For Paul, sin is a kind of bondage or servitude (e.g. 1 Corinthians 6.20). Christ has set us free, paid the purchase price – that is, 'redeemed' us, as we might redeem an item which we had pledged or pawned. Redemption, then, is not an airy-fairy technical term of theology, but a practical everyday business. We also find in scripture the idea that what Christ achieved on the cross was a deliverance from captivity by payment of a ransom (e.g. Revelation 5.9). We all know what a ransom is – someone is taken hostage; we have to pay a ransom to get them back. We were slaves to sin, and Christ bought us back with the price of his own blood. If we push this image to its natural human conclusion, it would suggest that the ransom of Christ's blood was paid to Satan, not to God. That was what some of the early Christians thought, although eventually the Church abandoned that idea. A good thing too, because when we try to imagine a ransom paid to Satan, our imagination is apt to fail us. Still, this is a valuable reminder that there are limits to how far even biblical metaphors, like ransom and redemption, can take us.

All the terms we have for describing the meaning of the crucifixion – satisfaction, ransom, redemption – are metaphorical. All of them preserve fragments of the complete meaning of the crucifixion. If we add to this list one more concept, we can draw as close as is humanly possible to the real heart of the atonement. That concept is *sacrifice*. We cannot understand the crucifixion, or formulate an understanding of atonement, without giving due weight to the practice of sacrifice, and how it works upon the mind and heart of the one seeking God. Sacrifice, however, is a much misunderstood term, and potentially misleading, so I need to make clear that I am thinking first of literal, blood sacrifice, not a metaphorical sacrifice. When we talk of sacrifices we usually mean metaphorical ones – giving up something valuable or precious, setting aside personal pleasure or convenience for the sake of some principle or good. But literal sacrifice is something so distant from our modern religious experience that it is hard for us to understand it at all. Literal sacrifice is the letting of blood through the ritual killing of a living creature, by which a change in relationship is wrought between God and his people. At the time of Jesus, sacrifice was the universal form of worship for both Jews and non-Jews; there was a common understanding that it was *the* way of approaching the divine. It bound people together through the ritual act and through the meal connected with it. This is undoubtedly what Paul (or his disciple) has in mind when he says of Christ, 'In him all the fullness of God was pleased to dwell, and through him God was pleased to reconcile to himself all things, whether on earth or in heaven, by making peace through the blood of his cross' (Colossians 1.19–20). This is the language of sacrifice. It might have been sneered at by the philosophical few as primitive and irrational but it was nonetheless universally practised and regarded as trustworthy and effective.

What did a sacrifice need to be made *for*, though? What was the balance that had to be restored? Well, we cannot escape from the reality of sin; denying a penal substitution theory of the atonement does not absolve us of the need to regard our sins and wrongdoing in a clear cold light, for what they truly are. For as the Book of Common Prayer confession puts it, 'we have left undone those things which we ought to have done: and we have done those things which we ought not to have done; and there is no health in us'. Yet is it not love, rather than fear, that calls forth our deepest sorrow for sin? Does not God desire contrition – a heart sorry for sin because of its love for God, and not attrition, a heart sorry for sin out of fear of punishment?

The stories of real people's experiences in the Gospels point us to the truth that recognizing Jesus for what he is sets in motion a series of 'recognitions' of human weakness and frailty. In the previous chapter, I used a number of biblical examples, such as Simon of Cyrene, Dismas the penitent thief and Thomas, to show what I think is a paradigm, an exemplar, of a right relationship between human beings and God, which amounts, in each instance I noted, to a 'recognition'. From the stories of others, and from our own experience, we also know that our moments of recognition may have to happen over and over again – as Peter had to recognize Jesus for what he truly was, not only at Caesarea Philippi, but also at his trial (through Peter's own betrayal and the crowing of the cock), and afterwards at his resurrection appearance (John 21.15–19), and then again in yet another way at Pentecost. This is how we come to recognition, to see God-in-Christ for what he is; and this is how we reach a true perception of our own unrighteousness, by contrast with his infinite goodness and mercy.

We know that the world is soiled by wickedness – the failings of ourselves as individuals, which we confess, Sunday by Sunday, and the corporate failings in which most of us are complicit most of the time, like the squandering of resources, the destruction of the environment, or global poverty. For all this – for the wickedness of individuals and groups – Jesus died. God did not punish Jesus for our sins, but he 'laid on him the iniquity of us all' (Isaiah 53.6). God gave the burden of the world's sin to Jesus, he laid it upon the shoulders of the only one able to bear it, because in Jesus the God-man, the Messiah, human sinfulness and the love of God are reconciled. He was wounded *for* our transgressions, bruised *for* our iniquities; but not because we are mired in sin, wallowing in our own wickedness. Sin should be recognized, confessed, and put away. To claim that our sins *made* God punish Jesus is pathetic pride.

We have now established the right basis of our relationship with God-in-Christ: not self-destroying guilt or fear or shame, but 'recognition' and, following on from that, contrition. All this can be summed up in the single word 'repentance'. Repentance has to be renewed over and over again, as we grow, as our understanding of God changes and develops. So we have begun to reach out for another way to understand the meaning of the crucifixion, but we have not finished the task. We still need to explore further how God was in Christ reconciling the world to himself.

To repeat what I said earlier, I believe, along with the first Christians, that the essence of the atonement, the key to understanding the meaning of the crucifixion, is sacrifice. In the Old Testament it was vital that the victim offered in a sacrifice be perfect (Exodus 12.5). Nothing but the best should be sacrificed to God. This perfection comes to be an essential element in the first Christians' understanding of the death of Jesus, as a 'lamb without blemish' (1 Peter 1.19). The author of the letter to the Hebrews explores this theme in greatest depth, showing how the imperfect sacrifices of an imperfect high priest had to be endlessly repeated, and were not completely effective. Only the true perfection of both priest and sacrificial victim meant that the sacrifice could be 'once for all' (Hebrews 9.15–28).

We might feel that understanding the atonement as a sacrifice is just as cruel and unjust as penal substitution. It is hard for us to imagine ourselves as part of a world where ritual killing and the pouring out of blood were believed to have power to cleanse sin and unite people to God. But when writers in the New Testament and the early Church describe the death of Christ as a perfect sacrifice, they are thinking about more than the killing of an animal. Of course the image of an innocent 'lamb to the slaughter' does have meaning – Paul remembers Psalm 44.22 and uses it in his account of salvation in Romans 8.31–39 – but the practical focus is on sacrifice as a means of sharing and uniting, a coming together through a common meal. In an era when meat was a rare luxury, a sacrifice meant a shared meal in the context of prayer and worship; it also meant an experience of God entering into human life at its most simple and basic, and becoming part of everyday existence, giving meaning to the ordinariness of life. In the end, of course, 'sacrifice' is just as much a metaphor as 'ransom' and 'redemption'. Such words are not used as *allegories* (which give a perfect and complete correspondence between sign and reality) but *images*, revealing glimpses of a reality beyond description. After all, an animal which is sacrificed has no choice, and no understanding; whereas we have already found that Jesus had both. It is probably inevitable that we cannot understand the image of sacrifice properly in our own culture, when meat comes wrapped in plastic from a supermarket and we can afford to eat it every day. We no longer expect that we shall have to grow or kill whatever food we eat.

None of this makes the idea of the Passion as a sacrifice easy to understand. But we can accept that the first Christians used the image of sacrifice when they tried to make sense of what had happened to Jesus. We can also shed new light on what sacrifice has become for later generations of Christians, especially, as we shall see below, when we think about the eucharist.

Paul teaches in Romans that Christ, the righteous one, undid the work of death which Adam's sin had inflicted on the world. So Jesus was, as one writer on atonement has argued powerfully, *Christus Victor* – the Victorious Messiah. His death is a victory over the grave, a conquest of death itself. His resurrection undoes the work of Adam's sin. But I am afraid this sort of talk is very unfashionable. Nobody these days wants a theory of atonement rooted in speculation about what is unseen and unprovable. Most people would rather stick to what they can see. Yet the Bible witnesses (especially through Paul) to the reality of a cosmic battle between good and evil: 'Then comes the end, when [Christ] hands over the kingdom to God the Father, after he has destroyed every ruler and every authority and power' (1 Corinthians 15.24; see also Romans 8.38). In this battle, Paul sees the faithful as conformed to the likeness of the crucified Lord, sharing with him in both his death and resurrection:

> Therefore we have been buried with him by baptism into death, so that, just as Christ was raised from the dead by the glory of the Father, so we too might walk in newness of life. For if we have been united with him in a death like his, we will certainly be united with him in a resurrection like his. We know that our old self was crucified with him so that the body

of sin might be destroyed, and we might no longer be enslaved to sin. For whoever has died is freed from sin. But if we have died with Christ, we believe that we will also live with him. We know that Christ, being raised from the dead, will never die again; death no longer has dominion over him. The death he died, he died to sin, once for all; but the life he lives, he lives to God. So you also must consider yourselves dead to sin and alive to God in Christ Jesus. (Romans 6.4–11)

It is very easy to be carried away by the power of Paul's words, but however exalted their expression may be, their meaning is perfectly plain. Through our baptism, we have already died to sin. We have not *caused* the crucifixion; we have *shared* in the crucifixion. Our old self has been crucified with him – that is, the self which had no 'recognition' of God. And we are already alive to God in Jesus Christ our Lord. Perhaps it is not surprising that Paul came to this view of the atonement. After all, he thought of himself as the chief of sinners, for God had worked in him despite his active hostility to the Gospel, and Christ had called him directly to the work of an apostle.

The death of Jesus is once for all, upon the cross. It is a cosmic event: an event which affects all human history for all time; which undoes the work of sin and death, and makes rebirth and renewal possible – what Paul calls 'newness of life'. It is not just exemplary – that is, it does not only teach us a lesson about love and goodness. It is *constitutive* – it makes a real, objective difference to how the world is, and to who and what we are. So we cannot simply say that Jesus died to encourage us to be self-sacrificing, to meet evil with love. That is true, but it is not enough. Many human beings have done likewise – not a few following in Jesus' footsteps. Some have died more dreadful deaths than Jesus. It is not the power of his example but the inner reality of the crucifixion itself which matters. The death of Jesus undoes death. His perfect offering of himself once for all, the lamb of God without spot or blemish, himself both priest and victim, changes reality.

I have said that the death of Jesus should not be understood as a metaphorical or figurative sacrifice (giving up what we value for the sake of some greater good) but as literal sacrifice (the ritual letting of blood of a living creature, and participation in its flesh, through which a union with the divine is brought about). There might seem to be a great gulf between these two uses of the one word 'sacrifice'; and yet, as it turns out, they may not be so far apart after all. When we speak of making sacrifices, we are really talking about letting go of part of ourselves, the death of some hope or dream or fantasy, some personal desire or pleasure, for the good of something or someone else. The same pattern is clearly discernible in both senses of 'sacrifice' – the letting go of life, in order to embrace life in all its fullness.

It may feel presumptuous or self-aggrandizing to think of one's own life in terms of sacrifice, and it is certainly best to avoid dwelling on whatever sacrificial good we have done, or evil we have patiently endured. There is a danger of lapsing into self-satisfaction, and so undoing all spiritual benefit, as Jesus knew when he advised, 'When you give alms, do not let your left hand know what your right hand is doing, so that your alms may be done in secret; and your Father who sees in secret will reward you' (Matthew 6.3–4). One of the most popular films of all time is a reflection of the theme of personal sacrifice, in which the hero is driven to suicidal despair, but led back to the path of life via a realization of the life-giving properties of his sacrifices. In *It's a Wonderful Life*, George Bailey (played by James Stewart) sees himself not as a hero but as a loser; he has no conception of the good his sacrifices have achieved until a crisis and a miracle make this evident.

Those sacrifices seemed trivial and insignificant, but their power is transformative; and the popularity of the film underlines how deeply the metaphor of sacrifice is imprinted on our self-understanding.

So perhaps there is something to be said after all for using our own personal experience of sacrifice to understand the crucifixion. We need more confidence in those practical experiences of sacrifice, so that we can draw on them when we attempt to understand the atoning sacrifice of Christ on the cross. We need to call to mind all the times when we have given up our own path, or surrendered our own will, for the good of others, or in response to the call of God – or those moments when we have found our own selfishness and self-centredness countered with love and self-sacrifice from others. Such moments can teach us the transformative power of sacrifice. And such sacrificial experiences are common to all peoples, not just to Christians.

The death of Christ is not, however, a metaphorical sacrifice, but a literal one. His real blood was really shed; his real life was really given up, to effect a transformation of relationship. There is one element in the religious experience of all Christians which connects us intimately with that literal sacrifice – holy communion. We need to pay greater attention to this actual experience of sacrifice. For every time we celebrate the eucharist, we are participating in a sacrifice. We do so in memory of him, as he commanded us: sharing the bread and wine, receiving the body and blood of Christ, so that we may become one with him. The relationship between this partaking of the sacrifice and being one body is clearly expressed in the words of the liturgy, which draw directly upon scripture – 'though we are many, we are one body, because we all share in one bread' (this is close to Romans 12.5: 'we, who are many, are one body in Christ, and individually we are members one of another'). Christ died for our sins, the just for the unjust, once for all; but he commanded us to recall and realize that sacrifice in our breaking of bread, and our sharing of the common cup.

We may find the notion of blood sacrifice in the worship of ancient Israel repellent, primitive, and even horrific. What has the ritual killing of animals to do with divine service in our nice, clean, dignified modern Church? But we should be clear what we are doing at the eucharist. Sacrifice is a universally understood religious language. Sacrifice restores and strengthens the bond between God and his people. 'For the life of the flesh is in the blood' (Leviticus 17.11) – life is given and shared to unite the whole community. In the eucharist, as Jesus commanded, we share in the flesh and blood, in the living sacrifice, and so are reconciled to God. For sacrifice is a means of effecting 'reconciliation' – which is how the word for 'atonement' is sometimes rendered (as in Romans 5.11).

I recall a woman saying to me after a eucharist long ago, 'Why do we have to say that awful Prayer of Humble Access? It's not nice for the children to read all that stuff about eating flesh and drinking blood.' But that is the irreducible meaning of Jesus' words, 'Unless you eat the flesh of the Son of Man and drink his blood, you have no life in you' (John 6.53). Through the sacrifice of a perfect victim, once for all, came perfect forgiveness. This is what Christians remember and receive through holy communion. Remember again the view of Judaism: 'the life of the flesh is in the blood'. No good Jew would willingly, knowingly, eat blood. It would be a terrible blasphemy to do so, a way of appropriating what belonged to God alone – life. But Jesus, a good, devout, law-abiding Jew, steeped in the Law's commands, gives his disciples the cup of wine and tells them: 'Drink from it, all of you; for this is my blood of the covenant, which is poured out for many' (Matthew 26.28; see also Mark 14.24; Luke 22.20).

If we want to understand the atoning sacrifice of Jesus on the cross, we have to take into account the sacrifice which he instituted on that night before he died. He has made this connection for us by his own words, imprinting the breaking of his body and the shedding of his blood onto the universal symbols of bread and wine. If we use our understanding of history and theology to tease out the meaning of the atonement, we come to an understanding in which Jesus' death is not only an example, and a satisfaction, and a ransom, and a redemption, but a perfect sacrifice, a means of grace which, by the body and blood (and for ever afterwards the bread and cup), effect unity between believers and the one in whom they believe. If this is right, the essence of the atonement is its power to unite through the blood of the cross – making us one. For all of us who are followers of Jesus, whenever we gather in church for worship, the eucharist is where this truth of the atonement is most completely realized on earth – however dreary the weather outside; however dreary the priest inside. The eucharist is still where we meet God. For us the eucharist is the eternal realization of that self-offering of Jesus made once for all upon the cross. The atonement is not just a theory, a label, a way of cobbling together bits of the Gospels: it is *real*.

So much for believers. In his wonderful providence God also uses sacrifice to disclose his reality to those who never come to church, and who have never met round the Lord's Table. Sacrifice is the essence of our common life as human beings – the ability to submit our own selves to the common good, to let go of what is valuable and precious for the sake of something greater. Every time we do so with a willing heart, we grow more Christ-like. This is what we see at work among soldiers in war who risk their own lives for the sake of fallen comrades, and sometimes even fallen enemies. We see it in families caring for loved ones who are sick, or disabled, or frail. Perhaps most strikingly, we see it in countless charitable organizations run by people who set aside their time and focus their abilities on the needs of others. They help because they can, and because of their belief that inequalities of talent, opportunity, health or circumstance need to be countered. The Christian message of sacrifice is so powerful because it answers to a universal, God-given human instinct. In the end, our belief in the justice of God is founded on an instinct to strive for justice for all, even at great cost to ourselves. This too is Christ-like.

In the penal substitution theory, God stood at a distance while Jesus paid the due penalty for sin and satisfied God's justice. Yet it is better to think of Jesus not as *substituting* himself for us, but rather *representing* us – just as Paul does when he calls him a second Adam (1 Corinthians 15.22). His death is not something which magically changes or reforms our relationship with God without our having to do anything ourselves. Instead it is something we must appropriate for ourselves, by being buried with him in baptism, and by taking up our own cross. So we must trust what the Gospel reveals to us – a view of the crucifixion and the atonement as sacrificial and triumphal, of God making the first move towards human-kind, in the incarnation, and, from this (as Paul teaches), achieving a cosmic victory over the powers of darkness. The crucifixion of Jesus is, at its heart, a sacrifice, which first makes, and then eternally renews, the covenant relationship of human beings with God.

At this point, at the end of the journey to the cross, there is briefly time for looking back. The sorrowful mysteries have led us from the agony in the garden to the scourging, the crowning with thorns, the carrying of the cross, and finally to the crucifixion. This story of the Passion speaks to all people for all time. It is not a mere history lesson, or a mere record of the past: it is a paradigm of our existence, and more than anything else it is a call to all people to take up their cross, and meet the challenges of life with passionate Christianity. I said at the beginning that the sorrowful mysteries were first of all a prayer. I pray them regularly, though often reluctantly, because it takes some courage to enter into the sorrow and suffering of Jesus. I say again that meditation is the best way for all of us to understand the Passion, and its meaning for us today. And I remind you that by 'meditation' I do not mean primarily *thinking about* God and Jesus; I mean using our imagination, and our spiritual awareness, to enter into the reality of our salvation, and so make the Gospel our own.

Paul said nearly two millennia ago that the message of the cross is folly to those who are perishing (1 Corinthians 1.18). And that has not changed. Without the eye of faith, the Passion is a beautiful, inspiring story – but only a story. It can have no objective meaning, no eternal significance. Yet even beautiful, inspiring stories sow seeds in human hearts, and those seeds can produce a rich harvest of love and sacrifice. Sometimes they can awaken faith as well. After all, how else could Christian faith be passed from one generation to the next? For those blessed with faith, the Passion is infinitely more than a story. To the eye of faith, the Passion discloses the nature and truth of God, and it does so in terms of an atoning sacrifice. It shows us the truth of the incarnation at work in human history – in Christ, God became human to make humanity divine; and it shows us the truth of the atonement – that Christ bore our sins in his own body on the tree, that we, being dead to sin, might live to righteousness (1 Peter 2.24). The Passion, therefore, acts as a commentary on the resurrection, making sense of the miracle of miracles.

For everyone who comes to believe in the resurrection, and who chooses to set out on the Lenten pilgrimage in the hope of encountering that miracle, the sorrowful mysteries can be a sign to the right path and also a way of understanding what is encountered on the journey to the cross:

At the end of the road, there stands the cross itself, as it has always done.

A pointer to the heavenly way.

A standard of victory.

A tree of life.

The sorrowful mysteries end with the crucifixion and death of Jesus. But the Passion story ends with the resurrection: with new life and with a new beginning.

Questions for further thought and discussion

1 Where did your Christian faith begin from?
2 What is the cornerstone, or the foundation, of your faith today?
3 Does the image of sacrifice make the crucifixion easier to understand, or harder?
4 Which person in the Passion story do you identify with most strongly, and (if you feel able to explain your reasons) why did you choose this person?

A prayer for the mystery of the crucifixion

God our Father,
standing at the foot of the cross
I look upon my crucified Lord.
In his Passion, help me to see the image of your love,
and so to offer my life in gratitude,
and in faithful trust that your service is perfect freedom,
through the same Jesus Christ our Lord. Amen.

References

Macquarrie, John, *Jesus Christ in Modern Thought* (London: SCM Press, 1990).

Milgram, Stanley, *Obedience to Authority: An experimental view* (London: Printer and Martin, 1997).

Paul VI, Pope, *Exhortation on Evangelization in the Modern World* (London: Catholic Truth Society, 2002).